This Is Life

This Is Life

Robert D. Brinsmead

Verdict Publications
Post Office Box 1311
Fallbrook, California 92028
U.S.A.

Library of Congress Catalog Card No. 78-59601

ISBN 0-89698-001-4

Printed in the United States of America

Dedication

To Judy, Paul, Sally and Daniel

Contents

Acknowledgments

I wish to thank the gentlemen who have placed their names on the introduction to this book. Their competence in various fields of health qualified them to give me much valuable assistance, especially in preparing the material for chapters two, three and four.

Introduction

This Is Life has grown out of a "how to live" seminar approach developed in Australia. Many will read this book by themselves with great profit. But we have found that using the book in small home-study groups can produce amazing results. Preferably, read one chapter each session, discuss it, and encourage each other to make at least one or two significant lifestyle changes. In subsequent sessions report on your pursuit of a better way of life. Mutual encouragement and group spirit work wonders. Then, at the end of the course, celebrate together. Arrange a reunion at a convenient date. If you use the book this way, you may be like many others who have said, "This is the greatest thing that has happened to my life."

D. Weston Allen, M.B., B.S., F.R.A.C.G.P.
Cedric L. Taylor, M.B., B.S.
Jack D. Zwemer, B.S., D.D.S., M.S., Ph.D.

1

The Pursuit of Life

Let us imagine that the treasure called life —life at its best, life as life was meant to be — is hidden on a great mountain peak. A path leads to it, and we are gathered at the starting point below. We are going to seek this treasure together. The time has come to begin, the prospects are hopeful, and we are eager to be off. Before we begin our journey, however, we need to know something about the path ahead. We need a clear, sound philosophy of life.

The Ideal Life

Our first and most fundamental definition of life —the ideal life —is that *life is being truly human.* It is as fussless and down-to-earth as that. If life is what we are after, we can forget about doing weird and wonderful things. Life is being truly human.

This raises a basic question. What does it mean to be truly human? One person looks for life in some exotic food, pill or potion, while another seeks it in meditation, and still another in social revolution. Each has a different view of life. The food faddist thinks man is basically a stomach on legs. The second person thinks man is a ghost in a machine. The third thinks of man as an economic animal. Each person's view of what man is determines his life and action.

We recognize that human nature is composed of various faculties. Among these are sight, hearing, speech, mobility, sexuality, affections and reason. But on reflection we see that these faculties have meaning only in the setting of relationships. Could there be any value to sight if there were nothing to see? What would be the use of speech if there were no one with whom to communicate? What of mobility if there were no place to go? Or of affections with no one to love? A mere description of faculties does not tell us what it means to be truly human. Our humanness is defined by our relationships, and therefore we are truly human only in our relationships. It is self-evident that we are related to the environment, to others and to ourselves.

To be human means being related to the environment in a certain way. It provides us with food to eat, places to go, and things to see and enjoy. To be human means having the capacity not only to react to our environment, but to act upon it.

To be human means being related to others. We are social creatures whose very existence rests on our solidarity with the human race. We are brought into the world by the action of others. The most independent person depends on others to service his needs. While we go about our own activities, others are growing our food, representing us in government, printing our newspapers and servicing an untold number of our daily needs. We switch on the light without even thinking that the activity of thousands of people who possess skills most of us know nothing about have made this possible.

Fred didn't want to be the slave of other people, so he made a million dollars. Now neither the alarm clock nor his wife could get him out of bed. "I don't have to work," he said. "I've made a million dollars." After he was weary of rest, he sauntered out to get his morning paper. There wasn't any. He went to get milk for his cornflakes. There was none. He turned on the television set to watch his favorite program. It was off the air. Nothing was working. The situation was desperate. What was the matter? Everybody had made a million dollars! Fred began to sweat. He was frantic. That awakened him, for it was only a dream. He got out of bed and went off content to serve his fellow men. Life would not only be dull and lonely, it would be impossible without others.

To be human means having a relationship with ourselves. While animals are conscious, only human beings are self-conscious. We have self-awareness. Either we have self-respect and a sense of self-worth, or we lack self-respect and believe we are worthless.

Human life is defined by relationships. We do not deny the reality of our faculties, but they have meaning only in the setting of relationships.

We are now ready to propose a second definition of life. *Life is being rightly related to the environment, to others and to ourselves.* We can call these three relationships physical, social and spiritual life.

Thinking relationally saves us from the mistake of dividing man into two or three distinct parts and then trying to look at each part separately. Human life is one. Each person is an indivisible unity. The physical, social and spiritual are not three different parts of the person. They are the same whole person seen from three different relationships. The whole person is a physical being. The whole person is a social being. And the whole person is a spiritual being. He is all three at the same time.

Since life is indivisibly one, whatever affects one relationship affects all relationships. If we mistreat our neighbor, we hurt our conscience — our sense of self-respect — and thus damage our spiritual life. If our diet is impoverished and we become irritable or diseased, we impair our social as well as our physical life. We cannot have well-being in one area of our existence unless we have well-being in every area. So we can say that life means to be *whole* in all our relationships. From the word *whole* come the words *wholesome* and *health*.

This brings us to a third definition of life. *Life is health.* By health we do not mean merely freedom from aches and pains, but wholeness and well-being of the total person. We could call it total health. So any time we talk about health or total health on our journey, let us remember we mean the same thing as life.

If life is a right relationship in all areas of human existence, this leads us logically to the next point. The moment we say *right* relationship we imply there is a distinction between right and wrong. Of course there is! There is a right and wrong way to relate to our environment. There is a right and wrong way to relate to others. And there is a right and wrong way to relate to ourselves.

What then is right and what is wrong? To which we must answer, right and wrong are defined by law. It is self-evident that we live in a structured universe governed by law. There are laws which guide the planets and other heavenly bodies in their courses. There are laws which relate to the lives of animals and man. Nothing we see in this world can escape the operation of law.

The universal laws which govern the world and everything in it have three features:

1. Law is a *given*. We didn't choose it or think it up. No person can decide within himself what a universal law shall be. It is objective. It is there whether we recognize it or not.

2. Law is *inexorable*. It never changes. It has no favorites. It is absolutely impartial and unvarying. Two plus two always equals four. A falling object always accelerates at a rate fixed by the law of gravity. Astronauts must make thousands of calculations based on invariable laws. If they do not re-enter the earth's atmosphere at the right angle and velocity, they are doomed. Without inexorable law an unpredictable world would make life impossible.

3. Law is *penal*. A penalty is always attached to its violation. There is a difference between law and advice. We may ignore advice without experiencing harm, for advice may or may not be based on law. But if we violate a fundamental law of life, we will suffer the consequences. If someone jumps off a tall building, the law of gravity will destroy him within seconds. He doesn't really break the law. The law breaks him. If another puts his hand on a hot stove, he will find an unalterable law which produces painful tissue destruction. An engineer knows that a piece of steel with certain specifications can carry a certain load. If a bridge collapses or a dam bursts, someone has miscalculated. These principles apply to all relationships. I cannot hit my neighbor in anger without damaging our relationship and my own self-respect. Likewise, if I despise myself I will suffer certain psychological consequences.

The violation of law always brings a penalty. We may suffer because of someone else's violation of the laws of life. But in most cases we have disregarded these laws ourselves. We have disrupted some vital relationship and thereby brought suffering upon our own heads.

We are now ready to state our fourth definition of life — life at its best. *Life is being in harmony with the unalterable laws of life.* Most of us would like to think we can find health in some more spectacular way. The humdrum business of bringing our lives into harmony with the unalterable laws of life requires discipline. We are tempted to think it is easier to take herbs and drugs or to undergo surgery. These, however, are measures to deal with disease. What we are talking about is health, not disease. Health is not found in remedies, good or bad. When some people are told that the basis of health is conformity to the laws of life, they groan, "Has it come to that?" They would rather empty their purses on an operation to remove a "guilty" organ, swallow some mysterious potion or run to the ends of the earth after a dubious health messiah.

There Are No Secrets

The essential principles of successful living are as plain and open as the sunlight. What we need to know to live healthy, happy and successful lives is available to all. It is the responsibility of everyone. There are no secrets.

What are the basic laws of life which govern our relationship to the environment, to others and to ourselves? Let us begin with the most obvious and reason from the known to the unknown.

We cannot live without the environment. From it we receive air, water, food and sunlight. A person can live about five minutes without air, five days without water, five weeks without food, and somewhat longer, of course, without sunlight.[1] Life depends on a good supply of pure air, clean water, good food and adequate sunlight. That is right input.

Now there must be right function. In order to enjoy life and health we need correct posture, regular exercise, adequate rest, regular and moderate habits, proper hygiene and, most important of all, right mental attitude — to the environment, to others and to ourselves.

Here, then, are the ten laws of life:

---

1. We are speaking only in round figures.

Input	**Function**
1. Pure air	5. Correct posture
2. Clean water	6. Regular exercise
3. Good food	7. Adequate rest
4. Adequate sunlight	8. Regular and moderate habits
	9. Proper hygiene
	10. Right mental attitude

These basic principles of life are self-evident and self-authenticating. That is why there are no secrets. These fundamental laws of life make sense, and they are so simple that anyone who can count can understand and remember them. But let's not think they are child's play.

The practice of these basic laws of life will do more to promote the quality and length of life than the best agencies known to science. Medical science has made marvelous contributions toward healing disease and easing human suffering. But it has not removed the appalling burden of such diseases as heart attack, cancer, stroke and mental illness. People must be educated and motivated to live in compliance with the fundamental laws of life if there is to be improvement in the quality and length of life.

We will see that the ten laws cover everything really important. We will also see that they are all interrelated. Correct breathing depends on good eating, correct posture, regular exercise, sufficient rest and a right mental attitude. Proper hygiene is related to air, water, food, sunlight and exercise. In fact, each law is related to every other law. The violation of one tends to the violation of all. Most important, proper compliance with any law depends on a right attitude to the environment, to others and to ourselves.

Summary

Let us summarize what we have learned about the ideal life:

First, life is being truly human.

Second, life is being rightly related to the environment, to others and to ourselves.

Third, life is health — wholeness.

Fourth, life is being in harmony with the unalterable laws of life.

The ten laws of life are:

	Input		Function
1.	Pure air	5.	Correct posture
2.	Clean water	6.	Regular exercise
3.	Good food	7.	Adequate rest
4.	Adequate sunlight	8.	Regular and moderate habits
		9.	Proper hygiene
		10.	Right mental attitude

If you wish to take a health appraisal test which illustrates the benefits of compliance with the laws of life, turn to "Healthful Habits" in the Appendix, pages 106-110.

2

The Prescription for Life: Input

As we ascend the mountain on our journey, the ten laws of life will mark our path. Learning these laws will cost us a little time, but we will be well rewarded. Compliance can add years to our life and life to our years.

We will divide our presentation of each law into three simple sections. First, we will state the *principle*. Second, we will discuss *problems* encountered in relating to each law. Third, we will get our *prescription*.

Law of Life 1: Pure Air

Principle. Our bodies need air. The blood must be constantly charged with oxygen. The 75 trillion cells of the body perform amazing physical, chemical and electrical feats, but without air these would quickly halt.

Life and health depend on pure air — lots of it. It imparts freshness to the skin, stimulates the appetite, aids the digestion, vitalizes the brain, soothes the nerves and invigorates the whole body.

Problem. Millions are deprived of vitality and life because they get neither the right *quality* nor *quantity* of air.

Nature has provided an ample supply of pure air, but man has polluted it.

> The *entire atmosphere* of our planet is now afflicted to some degree. Meteorologists talk about a nebulous veil of air pollution encircling the entire Earth. Smog has been observed over oceans, over the North Pole, and in other unlikely places. Mankind is taxing the capacity of the atmosphere to absorb and to transport away from areas of high population density the enormous amounts of waste exhausted into it. Air pollution is now recognized not only as an agent that rots nylon stockings and windshield wiper blades, that corrodes paint and steel, blackens skies and the wash on the clothesline, and damages $500 million worth of crops annually; it is recognized as a killer of people.[1]

Major causes of pollution are dust, smoke and fumes of industry and cities, motor vehicle exhaust and overcrowded, poorly ventilated rooms. Tobacco smoke is an especially dangerous form of air pollution. The well-known Framingham study has shown that a man 45-54 years of age who smokes more than 20 cigarettes a day has twice the risk of death from all causes as a nonsmoker the same age.[2]

A long list of such horrible diseases as cancer of the mouth, throat, lung and urinary bladder, as well as emphysema, heart disease and stroke, is not the only price to pay for this doubtful pleasure. What the smoker loses in present quality of life may be worse. A person who smokes two packs of cigarettes a day reduces the oxygen supply to the tissues of his body by 10% through the inhalation of the lethal gas, carbon monoxide.[3] Obviously, this is not going to improve either his mental or physical function.

The body is a beautiful, finely tuned mechanism. But the

---

1. P. R. Ehrlich and A. H. Ehrlich, *Population, Resources, Environment: Issues in Human Ecology,* 2nd ed. (San Francisco: W. H. Freeman & Co., 1972), pp. 146-47.

2. D. Shurtleff, "Some Characteristics Related to the Incidence of Cardiovascular Disease and Death: Framingham Study, 18-Year Follow-up," Section 30, *The Framingham Study: An Epidemiological Investigation of Cardiovascular Disease,* ed. W. B. Kannel and T. Gordon (Washington, D. C.: U. S. Government Printing Office, 1974), Table 12-9.

3. P-O. Åstrand and K. Rodahl, *Textbook of Work Physiology* (New York: McGraw-Hill Book Co., 1970), pp. 588-89.

smoker dulls its sensitivity to taste, smell and touch. He diminishes his enjoyment of life. He loses more time from work and is less efficient in his work.[4] A woman spoils her beauty by tobacco-stained teeth, a "granny chin" and prematurely wrinkled skin.[5] Those who do not smoke themselves — especially children of smoking parents — are made to suffer also.[6] This is because "sidestream" smoke contains many times more tars, chemicals and noxious gases than the smoke which the smoker inhales.[7]

The quantity of air is also crucial to life. The amount of air we breathe depends on how often we breathe and on the vital capacity[8] of our lungs. The Framingham study has shown that vital capacity is associated with length of life. For instance, a middle-aged man with a vital capacity of two liters — which is not uncommon — has at least three times the risk of death as a man the same age with a vital capacity of five liters.[9] A low vital capacity not only restricts our length of life, but our quality of life as well. The brain is first to be affected by an inadequate supply of oxygen. The intellect is dulled, the judgment impaired, and we tend to feel impatient and irritable. Moreover, the heart, stomach, liver and other vital organs suffer. Digestion is retarded and waste products are retained in the blood. Muscles become more tense and there may be general depression and sleepiness.

More information about pollution and vital capacity, however, will not change people's ways. Many who know the harmful effects of smoking continue smoking. Their real problem is mental attitude. They have a wrong attitude toward themselves. They

---

4. U.S. Department of Health, Education and Welfare, *The Health Consequences of Smoking: 1975* (Atlanta: Center for Disease Control, 1975), p. 5.

5. Department of Continuing Education, Harvard Medical School, *Harvard Medical School Health Letter* 3, no. 2 (1977): 1; L. E. Lamb, ed., "Tobacco: Cigarettes, Cigars, Pipes," *Health Letter* 2, no. 6 (1973): 3.

6. A. Brody and B. Brody, *The Legal Rights of Nonsmokers* (New York: Avon Books, 1977), pp. 13-42.

7. U.S.D.H.E.W., *Health Consequences*, p. 89.

8. Vital capacity is the volume of air that can be expelled from the lungs after taking a maximum breath.

9. D. Shurtleff, "Some Characteristics Related to the Incidence of Cardiovascular Disease and Death: Framingham Study, 16-Year Follow-up," Section 26, *The Framingham Study: An Epidemiological Investigation of Cardiovascular Disease* (1970), Tables 12-9-A, B.

are saying, "My life isn't worth much and my health isn't important." They do not value the life and health of others. And they do not value their environment.

Prescription. We all have a communal responsibility to reduce air pollution. And as far as possible we should live in an environment where the air is pure.

The best way to increase our vital capacity is to follow all the laws of life. Compliance in one area encourages compliance in the others. This means we should practice deep breathing[10] and speak from full inspirations of air. We should remove excess weight, maintain correct posture, get sufficient exercise, secure adequate rest, practice regularity and moderation and, most important of all, cultivate an attitude which sees value in ourselves, in others and in the environment. All relationships, including our relationship to the environment, deteriorate when we take them for granted.

Law of Life 2: Clean Water

Principle. Our body is about 70% water, our blood nearly 80%. Blood carries the food, enzymes, hormones and other chemicals to every part of our body. Watery fluids lubricate the joints of our body. Water removes body wastes and keeps our system internally hygienic. It is also useful in maintaining external cleanliness.

Our body needs about 1,500 gallons of water every day. Fortunately, it recycles most of this water. Otherwise we would have to drink at least 24,000 glasses a day. Some water is lost, however, and because of this we do need about six glasses a day in cool weather and more in hot weather or when doing vigorous exercise. Health depends on good, clean water, and lots of it.

Problem. Most of us do not drink enough water. Thirst is not always an accurate indication of our needs. A sedentary lifestyle and poor habits have accustomed many of us to a state of partial

---

10. See Appendix, "Healthful Deep Breathing," p. 111.

dehydration. This tends to cause fatigue, impairment of intellectual function, and constipation. The system also tends to collect impurities, which place a strain on the kidneys. Severe dehydration may seriously impair the heart and even cause death.[11]

Dr. G.C. Pitts and colleagues, of the Fatigue Laboratory at Harvard University, conducted some fascinating experiments with athletes exercising in a hot environment. When given enough water to quench their thirst, they could continue the same exercise nearly twice as long as when deprived of water. However, the athletes still drank one-third less water than they lost in sweat. When they drank the same amount of water as they lost in sweat, they showed no signs of heat exhaustion and felt they could continue exercising indefinitely.[12]

The quality of water is also a problem. Man seems bent on polluting the water in his environment. He pollutes the rivers, streams and water catchments with industrial wastes, herbicides, pesticides and other chemicals. In some countries, by poor hygiene and sanitation, he contaminates the water with dangerous bacteria which spread disease and death.

But the principal pollutants are those we ourselves add to water — like sugar, caffeine and alcohol. We would rather not accept the gift of pure water as man's best beverage. We insist on polluting it or changing it or making our own substitute. So again, the greatest problem is our attitude to the environment, to others and to ourselves.

Prescription. We should drink at least six glasses of water a day, and more in hot weather or when working hard. It isn't good to drink water at mealtimes. Diluting the digestive juices retards the process of digestion. So it is best to start the day with one or two glasses of water about half an hour before breakfast, with another generous amount at midmorning and midafternoon. That "all gone," exhausted feeling between meals might not be

---

11. Food and Nutrition Board, Division of Biological Sciences, Assembly of Life Sciences, National Research Council (prepared by the Committee on Nutritional Misinformation), National Academy of Sciences, May 1974, "Water Deprivation and Performance of Athletes," *American Journal of Clinical Nutrition* 27 (1974): 1096-97.

12. G.C. Pitts, R.E. Johnson and F.C. Consolazio, "Work in the Heat As Affected by Intake of Water, Salt and Glucose," *American Journal of Physiology* 142 (1944): 253-59.

from lack of food. We may simply need a glass of water.

The ten laws of life are interrelated. Compliance with one tends toward compliance with the others. Exercise, for instance, will prompt us to drink more water. Drinking more water, however, is largely a habit. And developing this habit depends on a right mental attitude.

Law of Life 3: Good Food

Principle. Our bodies are sustained by the products of the earth. The principle of a good diet may be simply stated: Food needs to be of the right kind, eaten in the right amount, at the right time and in the right frame of mind.

The ideal diet is composed of foods as near as possible to their natural state. This includes a generous variety of fruits, vegetables and whole grains. If we eat an ample variety of natural foods, we won't have to measure vitamins, minerals, fiber or protein. Our body will extract just what it needs for maximum strength and endurance.

The right amount of food is that which maintains our body at its desirable weight.[13] Studies have shown that it is better to be 10% overweight than 10% underweight.[14] Nature allows the comfort of a little leeway, so there is no need to be obsessed with acquiring a lean, hungry look.

In normal circumstances food should be eaten no more than three times a day and at regular intervals. It is better to eat a substantial breakfast[15] and a light meal in the evening. In this way more calories are burned during the day, and the body is

---

13. See Appendix, "Healthful Weight," pp. 112-13.

14. N.B. Belloc and L. Breslow, "Relationship of Physical Health Status and Health Practices," *Preventive Medicine* 1 (1972): 409-21; N.B. Belloc, "Relationship of Health Practices and Mortality," *Preventive Medicine* 2 (1973): 67-81; Shurtleff, "Framingham 18-Year Follow-up," Table 12-6; G. V. Mann, "Obesity—The Affluent Disorder," *Southern Medical Journal* 70 (1977): 902-3.

15. W.W. Tuttle and E. Herbert, "Work Capacity with No Breakfast and a Mid-Morning Break," *Journal of the American Dietetic Association* 37 (1960): 137-40.

better able to maintain its blood-sugar level under stress. Furthermore, a person sleeps better when his stomach is resting.

Food should be eaten in the right frame of mind. A sour mind can make a sour stomach. A poor mental attitude often accompanies poor digestion. On the other hand, if a person believes his food will do him good, it probably will. Peace, contentment, thankfulness and love should be our companions at the meal table. The social, cultural and esthetic atmosphere for eating is also important. Eating should be a pleasant social occasion. Food should be attractively served. It should not only look good but taste good.

Problem. We do not always eat the right kind or the right amount of food, and we often eat at the wrong time and in the wrong frame of mind.

Most dietary problems in developed societies stem from eating too much refined and processed foods, fatty foods, stimulating or intoxicating foods, and food additives.

Refined and processed foods include sugar, white flour, polished rice and refined oils. These are not poisonous, and there is no evidence they cause harm when eaten sparingly. The real problem is threefold:

1. These foods are deficient in essential vitamins and minerals. Their excessive use can cause serious illness.

2. Foods high in sugar may have an unusual effect on eating patterns. Because they taste good and because they lack the bulk which helps appease the appetite, it is easy to eat too much of them. This tends to obesity,[16] to tooth decay, and can contribute to other health problems.

3. These foods lack fiber — roughage — essential for healthy bowel action.

---

16. *"obesity* . . . an increase in body weight beyond the limitation of skeletal and physical requirement, as the result of an excessive accumulation of fat in the body" *(Dorland's Illustrated Medical Dictionary,* 25th ed. [Philadelphia: W. B. Saunders, 1974]).

It is estimated that the average American secures 24% of his total calories from sugar.[17] This is much more than desirable. The average American also secures about 42% of his total caloric intake from fat.[18] Evidence indicates that this is much too high as well. Furthermore, the proportion of saturated fats and cholesterol is too high.[19] Red meats, butter and certain cheeses are high in saturated fats. Egg yolk, brains, kidneys, liver and butter are high in cholesterol.

A high fat intake reduces physical endurance and contributes to the problem of obesity.[20] In addition, a high fat intake, particularly of saturated fats and cholesterol, has been linked to a higher risk of death from heart and artery disease.[21] Excessive fat may also be a factor in the development of bowel and breast cancer.[22]

Perhaps the most common stimulant is caffeine in coffee, tea and cola drinks. Caffeine is a potent stimulant of the central nervous system, but the sensation of alertness which it generates is not genuine. It can also be harmful to the heart, blood pressure, heart rate, muscle action and coordination, as well as to the stomach, digestion and kidneys.[23] We would be better off without dependence on caffeine.

---

17. United States Senate, *Dietary Goals for the United States,* prepared by the staff of the Select Committee on Nutrition and Human Needs (Washington, D.C.: U.S. Government Printing Office, 1977).

18. Ibid.

19. Ibid.

20. R. Passmore and J.S. Robson, eds., *A Companion to Medical Studies,* vol. 1, *Anatomy, Biochemistry, Physiology and Related Subjects* (Oxford: Blackwell Scientific Publications, 1968), pp. 42-3; T.S. Danowski, S. Nolan and T. Stephan, "Obesity," *World Review of Nutrition and Dietetics* 22 (1975): 270-79.

21. R. Masironi, "Dietary Factors and Coronary Heart Disease," *Bulletin World Health Organization* 42 (1970): 103-14; W.E. Connor and S.L. Connor, "The Key Role of Nutritional Factors in the Prevention of Coronary Heart Disease," *Preventive Medicine* 1 (1972): 49-83; K.P. Ball and R. Turner, "Editorial: Realism in the Prevention of Coronary Heart Disease," *Preventive Medicine* 4 (1975): 390-97; F. Young, "Diet and Coronary Heart Disease: Report of the Advisory Panel of the British Committee on Medical Aspects of Food Policy (Nutrition) on Diet in Relation to Cardiovascular and Cerebrovascular Disease," *Nutrition Today* 10 (1975): 16-27.

22. E.L. Wynder, "The Epidemiology of Large Bowel Cancer," *Cancer Research* 35 (1975): 3388-94; B.S. Reddy, A. Mastromarino and E.L. Wynder, "Further Leads on Metabolic Epidemiology of Large Bowel Cancer," *Cancer Research* 35 (1975): 3403-6; P. Stocks, "Breast Cancer Anomalies," *British Journal of Cancer* 24 (1970): 633-43.

23. L.E. Lamb, "Coffee, Tea, Cola, Cocoa," *Health Letter* 1 (1972): 1-4.

Although alcohol can be regarded as a food because of its high caloric value, it is in reality a mind-altering substance and therefore a drug. Taken in excess, alcohol plays havoc with the individual drinker and with the community. Not only does alcohol create enormous mental and social problems, but it is also a significant factor in cirrhosis of the liver, in cancer of the throat, mouth and liver, in certain forms of heart disease and in malnutrition.[24] Unborn infants of drinking mothers also suffer great risk of severe and permanent injury. Alcoholism has become a terrible curse to modern society.

Rats placed on a good diet preferred water to alcohol. However, given the poor quality of food found in a typical American diet, they began drinking alcohol. When spices and coffee were added to this diet, the rats doubled their alcohol intake. Returned to a good diet free of spices and caffeine, they abandoned alcohol within a week. But three weeks after recommencing an "alcoholic" diet, the rats were back to their old habits.[25] How many alcoholics are created at the meal table?

Food additives are another problem. Hundreds of preservatives, fortifying agents, colorings, flavorings, moisturizers and texturizers are added to processed foods. Some additives have been shown to be a health risk and have been banned by government action.[26] Others are suspect.

Common table salt is the food additive causing the greatest problem in many countries. Some salt is necessary, but most of us eat far too much.[27] Excessive salt intake has been linked to an

24. M. E. Chafetz, *Alcohol and Health: Second Special Report to the U.S. Congress* (Rockville, Md.: Alcohol, Drug Abuse and Mental Health Administration, National Institute on Alcohol Abuse and Alcoholism, 1974); idem, "How Alcohol Affects Your Health," *Medical News* 1, no. 20 (1977): 10-11.

25. U. D. Register, S. R. Marsh, C. T. Thurston, B. J. Fields, M. C. Horning, M. G. Hardinge and A. Sanchez, "Influence of Nutrients on Intake of Alcohol," *Journal of the American Dietetic Association* 61 (1972): 159-62.

26. N. Sapeika, "Food Additives," *World Review of Nutrition and Dietetics* 16 (1973): 334-62.

27. L. E. Lamb, ed., "Salt Linked to High Blood Pressure," *Health Letter* 9 (1977): 1; idem, ed., "Salt: Your Vital Sodium and Potassium Balance," ibid. 10 (1977): 1-4.

increased incidence of high blood pressure.[28] This is a major factor in heart attacks and strokes as well as in other serious health problems.[29]

Some food processing is necessary, and a few additives are perhaps better than stale or moldy foods. But most of us would benefit from eating much less refined, processed and fatty foods, stimulating or intoxicating foods, and food additives. These should be replaced with more fresh vegetables and fruits.

Obesity increases the risk of death from cardiovascular disease.[30] Obesity is often associated with eating too much sugar or butter, margarine, oils and other fats. It may also be related to eating at the wrong time and in the wrong frame of mind.

Too many persons eat just one meal a day — all day. Between-meal snacks disturb the regular digestive process and often contribute to overweight.

Many people would lose weight if they simply ate their evening meal for breakfast and their breakfast in the evening. More calories would be burned during the day instead of being stored as fat at night. As one wag has said, "Breakfast is golden, lunch is silver, and supper is lead."

What eats us is often far more important than what we eat. Worry, guilt, hostility, fear and hate can turn good food into poison. They may also turn us into compulsive eaters. While some console themselves with alcohol, others console themselves with food. Lack of self-respect and of a true sense of self-worth makes us indifferent to our health and reckless in our habits. But it is just as bad to become obsessed and preoccupied with food. We aren't all stomach, and neither is life.

Prescription.[31] The main dietary recommendations have already been suggested. Man's ingenious technology has not been able to improve upon the products of the earth. Most people need

---

28. G. R. Meneely and L. K. Dahl, "Electrolytes in Hypertension: The Effects of Sodium Chloride," *Medical Clinics of North America* 45 (1961): 271-83; L. K. Dahl, "Salt and Hypertension," *American Journal of Clinical Nutrition* 25 (1972): 231-44.
29. Shurtleff, "Framingham 18-Year Follow-up."
30. Ibid.
31. See Appendix, "Healthful Diet," pp. 114-15.

to eat much more fruit, vegetables and whole grains containing starch and fiber, and much less refined sugar.

Most people also need to eat much less fat and cholesterol.[32] Fats should preferably be eaten as they occur naturally rather than in fatty spreads, dressings and oils. Unsaturated fats may well be preferable to hard fats.[33] But even polyunsaturated vegetable oils should be used in moderation.

Such foods as potatoes and plain wholemeal bread are not fattening. A person would have to eat more than 20 potatoes or 30 slices of wholemeal bread a day just to maintain normal body weight. It is the dollops of cream, butter, margarine and oil added to these foods which make them high in calories. A teaspoon of butter or margarine contains nearly as many calories as a slice of bread but is not nearly as filling.

Added salt and salty foods should be restricted. Caffeine beverages, and alcoholic beverages in particular, should be discouraged.

Above all, the whole diet question must be viewed in the setting of the other laws of life. We must remember the principle that compliance with one law of life tends to compliance with the others. Exercise has a moderating effect on the diet. Regular and moderate habits are also important to diet. But a right mental attitude is most important of all. In eating our food, there is no better advice than that given long ago by Solomon, "Better a dish of vegetables with love than the best beef served with hatred."

Law of Life 4: Adequate Sunlight

Principle. There can be no life without light. Ultraviolet radiation from sunlight converts certain natural oils in or on the skin to vitamin D. This is rapidly absorbed into the blood. Vitamin D then helps the body use calcium, which is necessary for the bones,

---

32. U.S. Senate, *Dietary Goals,* pp. 30, 37.

33. I.S. Wright and D.T. Fredrickson, "Primary Prevention of the Atherosclerotic Diseases: Report of Inter-Society Commission for Heart Disease Resources," *Circulation* 42 (1970): A84-A87.

teeth, muscles and nerves. Ultraviolet rays may also benefit a number of skin conditions such as psoriasis, acne, boils and impetigo. Each year thousands of infants are successfully treated for jaundice of the newborn, with light as the only therapy.[34]

Research suggests that sunlight helps synchronize the fundamental biochemical rhythms of the body.[35] Natural sunlight has a relaxing effect on the nerves. And it does something for the spirit as well.

Problem. Artificial light is not an adequate substitute for sunlight. We need natural sunlight.[36]

We injure our health when we get either too much sunlight or not enough. Without adequate sunlight people are more prone to depression. On the other hand, too much sunlight can cause premature aging and wrinkling of the skin. In addition, excessive exposure to sunlight is often associated with skin cancer.

Prescription. We should try to get at least a few minutes of direct sunlight on the hands and face each day. By exercising in the open air we can secure necessary sunlight and practice several laws of life at once. We need, however, to protect our skin from too much harsh summer sun, particularly in the middle of the day. This is especially important for people with fair skin who live in tropical areas.

The rooms of the house should be exposed to sunlight — nature's antiseptic — especially during periods of warm moist weather and in winter. This will help eliminate house mites, molds, bacteria and other causes of respiratory allergies and infections.

Sunlight is an appropriate symbol for a cheerful spirit. Let's make good use of both.

---

34. R. J. Wurtman, "The Effects of Light on the Human Body," *Scientific American* 233 (1975): 68-79.
35. Ibid.
36. Ibid.

3

The Prescription for Life: Function

We trust our journey has been profitable and enjoyable so far. We will now learn five more laws of life. By complying with them we should come through feeling and looking better.

Law of Life 5: Correct Posture

Principle. Good posture is fundamental to proper development of body structure, especially of the bones and muscles. It aids the development of vital capacity and promotes deep breathing. It also encourages the circulation of blood to and from the heart. An erect bearing not only benefits physical health, but it lifts the spirits and promotes mental alertness and the dignity of self-possession. Physical posture is often a reflection of mental attitude.

Problem. A stiff, military-like posture and a slouched or drooping posture are both unhealthful. The stiff, precise posture puts an unnatural strain on the muscles.[1] A prolonged crouched or

---

1. L. E. Morehouse and L. Gross, *Total Fitness in 30 Minutes a Week* (New York: Pocket Books, 1975), pp. 18-19.

hunched position leaves the lungs with inadequate room to expand. It causes shallow breathing, reduces vital capacity and puts strain on the heart. It depresses and unbalances the circulation and contributes to headache, backache and aching neck, legs and feet. Poor posture is also associated with constipation and varicose veins. Moreover, it has an adverse psychological effect. It often accompanies feelings of inadequacy, hopelessness and depression.

Prescription. Good posture starts with the head, neck and trunk. The head should be up as if linked to a star. The neck should feel lengthened, the shoulders wider, and the upper spine of the trunk longer. Every activity should be accompanied by a sense of maximum lengthening of the spine. By concentrating on the head, neck and upper trunk, the rest of the body will tend to an erect, at-ease and balanced posture.[2]

Good posture is not only related to our positions while inactive, but to the positions we assume while working. Correct lifting of heavy objects, for instance, can help prevent injury and low back pain.

When lifting heavy objects, we can reduce pressure on the spinal disks by keeping the trunk as erect as possible. This involves bending the knees, putting the load on the leg muscles and keeping the weight as close to the body as possible. In this situation we should also take a deep breath and tense the abdominal muscles so that the increased pressure in the abdomen and chest will help support the rib cage and spine. This can significantly reduce the pressure on the lower back.[3]

The best way to develop good posture is to practice all the laws of health. Proper breathing and nutrition as well as adequate sleep will help us maintain an erect bearing. Adequate exercise will strengthen the muscles and skeleton. Ideally, we should be on our feet at least several hours a day.

We should strive for good posture until it becomes a regular habit. But an erect bearing requires an attitude of adequacy and

---

2. See Appendix, "Healthful Posture: Standing," p. 116; Personal communication from Dr. William Wilkie.

3. See Appendix, "Healthful Posture: Lifting and Carrying," p. 117. Those with special postural or skeletal problems should consult a physician.

self-esteem. We should walk tall like a thoroughbred, not arrogantly, but in recognition of the value and dignity of human life.

Law of Life 6: Regular Exercise

Principle. Every part of the body is made for action. Activity tends to life, inactivity to death. Doing nothing is the nearest thing to dying. Far more people die from want of exercise than from overfatigue. Exercise does wonders for the brain, the nerves, the heart, the veins and arteries, the circulation of the blood, the digestion, and the action of the liver, kidneys and lungs. It would be difficult to sufficiently laud its many benefits.

There are three basic types of exercise: calisthenic, isometric and aerobic. Calisthenic exercise is the stretching type. It improves the posture, relaxes the body and prepares for more vigorous activity. Isometric exercise makes one muscle strain against an immovable object or against another muscle, as when clenching the fists or cupping the hands together and pulling. This builds muscle strength but does little to improve general fitness. It can increase blood pressure and should therefore be avoided by those inclined to cardiovascular problems. Aerobic exercise moves whole masses of muscles, as in walking, swimming, cycling, running and active working. This is the best type of exercise.

In vigorous aerobic exercise the circulation of the blood through the heart and lungs may increase five times, and nearly twenty times through the working muscles.[4] Regular aerobic exercise has a beneficial training effect on the heart. It becomes stronger and more efficient, delivering more blood with each beat. With regular exercise the resting heart rate may be reduced from 72 to around 60 beats a minute. This saves nearly 6,000 beats a night and rests the heart as well as the body.

Problem. In societies where man cultivates and gathers his own food, using his legs instead of wheels, getting regular exercise is no problem. But it is a serious problem in other societies. Many of

---

4. Åstrand and Rodahl, *Textbook of Work Physiology,* p. 131.

us get neither enough exercise nor the right kind of exercise. This can contribute to obesity, high blood pressure, high blood-fat levels and a higher risk of heart disease.[5] Inadequate exercise also deprives many people of an important means of dissipating stress, resisting depression and maintaining a right mental attitude.

Prescription. We should find ways of increasing our level of activity when performing the necessary duties of life. For example, we could leave our car some distance from the office and walk to work. We could take the stairs instead of the elevator. We could find excuses to stand, stretch, move, swing or climb. Going for a walk during coffee break and romping with the children when we get home would also be a good idea. We were made to move. Let's shake off the tendency to inactivity. When we feel the need to exercise, we should not lie down until the feeling passes off. Let's become active and begin to live.

The simplest and safest form of exercise is walking, and it is very effective. Never begin a jogging program without first walking at least a few weeks. If you have a medical problem or are over 30, it is a wise precaution to have a thorough medical examination before undertaking a regular exercise program. An adequate exercise program will have a training effect on your heart, blood vessels and blood circulation.[6]

In this matter of exercise there is a close interrelation of the ten laws of life. Exercise helps us comply with the first law by encouraging correct breathing. When we exercise we tend to drink more water. Exercise also tends to moderate the appetite and

---

5. D.W. Allen and B.M. Quigley, "The Role of Physical Activity in the Control of Obesity," *Medical Journal of Australia* 2 (1977): 434-38; G.F. Fletcher and J.D. Cantwell, *Exercise in the Management of Coronary Heart Disease* (Springfield, Ill.: C.C. Thomas, 1971); E.C. Hammond and L. Garfinkel, "Coronary Heart Disease, Stroke, and Aortic Aneurysm," *Archives of Environmental Health* 19 (1969): 167-82; H.J. Montoye, H.L. Metzner, J.B. Keller, B.C. Johnson and F.H. Epstein, "Habitual Physical Activity and Blood Pressure," *Medicine and Science in Sports* 4 (1972): 175-81; R.S. Paffenbarger and W.E. Hale, "Work Activity and Coronary Heart Mortality," *New England Journal of Medicine* 292 (1975): 545-50; W.B. Kannel, P. Sorlie and P. McNamara, "The Relation of Physical Activity to Risk of Coronary Heart Disease: The Framingham Study," *Symposium: Coronary Heart Disease and Physical Fitness,* ed. O.A. Larsen (Baltimore: University Park Press, 1971).

6. See Appendix, "Healthful Exercise," pp. 118-19.

helps achieve normal body weight. If performed outdoors, it pro-vides the added benefit of sunlight. It promotes good posture, relaxation and sound, refreshing sleep. The discipline of the body in a routine of regular exercise also encourages a well-ordered lifestyle. Exercise helps expel impurities through the skin, kid-neys and bowels, and is indispensable to body hygiene. Most important, exercise promotes mental vitality, learning perform-ance and a healthy mental outlook. While exercise may seem irksome at first if we are not used to it, after a while it becomes a pleasure. When enjoyed, it does us more good.

Law of Life 7: Adequate Rest

Principle. None of us can live healthfully without adequate rest. It is essential for relaxation, recuperation, recreation and working efficiency. During rest and sleep the body and mind are restored and invigorated.

Rest needs to be in the right amount and of the right kind. Adults need seven or eight hours of sleep each day. Besides this, we need to break the cycle of work by laying aside the respon-sibilities of life for one full day each week. This practice is as old as human history. There are no reasons to question its benefit. It renews and enables us to take up the challenges and stresses of daily living.

The quality of rest is just as important as the quantity. We all know something about the benefits of sound, refreshing sleep.

Problem. Those who sleep five hours or less have nearly twice the death rate of people who regularly enjoy seven to eight hours of sleep.[7] Sleep deprivation also impairs judgment, reduces work capacity and increases the likelihood of errors. It weakens moti-vation and increases the energy required to perform a given task.[8]

---

7. E.C. Hammond, "Some Preliminary Findings on Physical Complaints from a Pro-spective Study of 1,064,004 Men and Women," *American Journal of Public Health* 54 (1964): 11-23.

8. W.B. Webb, *Sleep: An Experimental Approach* (New York: Macmillan Co., 1968), pp. 18-21.

The quality of sleep is often impaired by improper breathing, poor nutrition, late suppers, lack of exercise, overwork, irregular hours for retiring and — contrary to general opinion — by sleeping pills. Excessive use of sleeping pills actually disturbs sleep and is detrimental to life and health.[9] Most of all, sleep is destroyed by a wrong mental attitude. Greed, selfishness, guilt, worry, fear and hate can rob us of proper rest.

Prescription. Practicing the laws of life will help form better sleeping habits. Deep breathing and adequate fresh air promote sound sleep. Regular meals, exercise, and hard work according to our strength also encourage sleep. Solomon said, "Sweet is the sleep of the working man." Other aids to sleep include practicing moderation in everything, burying worry, guilt and negative thoughts, and living at peace with ourselves and others.

Law of Life 8: Regular and Moderate Habits

Principle. We all have a built-in biological clock or circadian rhythm. This daily rhythm is acquired very early in life and is important to the health and well-being of man. Physical and mental efficiency, alertness and skill are closely related to this biological rhythm.[10]

Health depends on good habits practiced with regularity and moderation. While regularity means doing things at the right time, moderation means doing things in the right amount. It means proportion, balance and the avoidance of extremes.

The daily routine of a well-ordered lifestyle poses less stress for the human organism. But even here we need moderation or life will become too regimented. Order needs a dash of variety. Routine should make room for a human touch of flexibility. Then discipline can be truly beautiful.

---

9. M.W. Johns, "Sleep and Hypnotic Drugs," *Drugs* 9 (1975): 448-78.

10. N. Kleitman, *Sleep and Wakefulness,* 2nd ed. (Chicago: University of Chicago Press, 1963), pp. 131-92; J.D. Palmer, *An Introduction to Biological Rhythms* (New York: Academic Press, 1976).

Problem. Human nature is vulnerable to irregularity. Our fitful starts at self-improvement do not establish good habits. We find it easy to become addicted to harmful things and to use good things in excess. Our society is satiated with overindulgence. In the developed countries more people die from too much food than from too little. We rust out from laziness more than we wear out from exercise. Too many of us are overfed, overstimulated, overmedicated, overstressed and underdisciplined. But the real problem is a wrong mental attitude. Bad habits are usually an expression of an unconscious sense of self-contempt and self-hate.

Prescription. We should practice each law of life regularly until it becomes an established habit, shunning that which is harmful, avoiding extremes and enjoying moderation in those things which are lawful. Above all, we need to cultivate a sense of self-respect and to pursue a worthwhile goal and purpose in life.

Law of Life 9: Proper Hygiene

Principle. Hygiene means to maintain ourselves and our environment in a manner which promotes health. In this we have a responsibility not only to ourselves but to others. Proper hygiene cannot be maintained merely by individual action. It demands the cooperation of every person. Each must contribute to the common good by doing his part to maintain himself and the environment in a healthful condition.

Man was made to exercise dominion over his environment, not to let it dominate him. In order to sustain life it is necessary for us to use our environment. We must develop our water resources and cultivate the soil to produce our food. Proper hygiene will not abuse the environment but will maintain it in a way that promotes health.

The practice of good hygiene means keeping ourselves and the environment clean, orderly and attractive. This makes it easier to keep the other laws of life. Cleanliness is vital if we are to have pure air, clean water, good food and adequate sunlight. It even contributes to adequate rest. Orderliness also helps insure correct eating, exercising and resting. An attractive environment in the company of attractive persons improves our attitude and imparts a general sense of health and well-being. In fact, proper mental hygiene — the maintenance of wholesome attitudes — is almost impossible if we or our surroundings are dirty, disorderly and unattractive.

Problem. While every human being knows that the world was meant to be clean, orderly and attractive, we must face the fact that it is not. Where nature has been left untouched by man, it possesses these attributes in all their loveliness. But man has befouled himself and polluted his environment. We have no one to blame but ourselves. We have sadly failed to exercise proper dominion over ourselves and over nature. We have abused and exploited our environment rather than using and maintaining it.

Pollution is a universal problem. Among some, pollution consists in the human and animal filth that is allowed to accumulate. Among others, the pollution is even more dangerous. Air, water, soil, food and sunlight have all been affected by industrial and urban waste, by heavy metals and exotic chemicals, and by invisible radiation.[11]

While modern hygiene and sanitation have done much to rid the earth of terrible scourges such as the Black Death, they have not changed man's insatiable urge to defile himself and his world. Man's real problem is in his mind, in his attitudes, not in his circumstances, activities and industries.

Prescription. In this matter of proper hygiene we can make some specific recommendations:

We should do our part to keep the environment we share with others as hygienic as possible.

We should locate ourselves and our families in areas that are as free as possible from pollution and congestion. The polluted air, congestion and noise of the city are not as hygienic as a good rural environment.

We should keep our premises clean, not allowing decaying animal or vegetable matter around our homes. Our environment

---

11. Ehrlich and Ehrlich, *Issues in Human Ecology,* pp. 145-92.

should also be kept orderly and attractive. This will not only provide physical exercise, but a restful atmosphere that promotes right mental attitude.

Our own persons must be kept clean, orderly and attractive. The reward will be better health, a clearer, more energetic mind, and the esteem and friendship of others.

The best prescription for hygiene is compliance with the other laws of life. The body cannot be internally hygienic without pure air, clean water, good food, adequate sunlight, correct posture, exercise, rest, and regular and moderate habits. Most important of all, we should cultivate an attitude that will lead us to relate in a responsible way to our personal hygiene and to the environment around us.

4

The Value of Life

Law of Life 10: Right Mental Attitude

We trust that climbing the path toward life has not proved too difficult thus far. In fact, we hope it has been a pleasure. We come now to the last law of life: right mental attitude. It is a big one. It is so important that we need a general orientation. Then in succeeding stages of our ascent we will deal with the principle, the problem and the prescription for right mental attitude.

The possession of health information alone will not bring better health. Society is saturated with such information. We know more about the dangers of polluted air and water, about good nutrition and the benefits of exercise, than any other generation has ever known. But that does not stop people from smoking and watching television until their bodies nearly rot for want of exercise. Reformation must spring from the center of human existence. We sometimes call this center the heart. Long ago a wise Oriental king said, "As a man thinks in his heart, so is he."

Mental attitude undergirds and controls all other life factors. We have seen that wrong mental attitude is the major cause of air, water and food pollution. Indeed, wrong mental attitude is the greatest factor in all our reckless, self-destructive habits. Someone has said, "We are not what we think we are, but what we think, we are." The way we think determines our actions, good or bad.

More than half the illnesses from which people suffer have their foundation in the mind. Popular books have familiarized us with psychosomatic illness.[1] Hate, grief, guilt, discontent, fear and other destructive thought patterns affect the heart, blood, stomach, digestion, liver, nerves and hormones, making us vulnerable to a host of illnesses. Scientific studies have explored the relationship of stress to heart attacks, stomach ulcers, asthma, cancer and other diseases.[2] The evidence points in one direction: Happy, well-adjusted people tend to live longer and suffer less disease. A study conducted at Duke University showed that work satisfaction and personal happiness were far more significant to the length of life than were all other factors, including physical functioning and tobacco use.[3]

Of course, we need to remember that cause and effect work both ways. Physical habits have a profound effect on the mind too. The air we breathe, the water we drink, our nutrition, our exposure to sunlight, our posture, exercise, rest, moderation and hygiene — all have a vital bearing on mental health. And this in turn reacts upon the body.

Trying to determine whether some ailments originate in physical or in mental habits is often pointless. Human life is one. The idea that body and mind — or body and soul — are two separate, distinct entities is an erroneous and damaging philosophy. Originating in ancient Greece, it made its way into Western thinking and often found nourishment, of all places, in the Chris-

-----

1. "*psychosomatic* . . . [*psycho-* mind + Gr. *soma* body] pertaining to the mind-body relationship; having bodily symptoms of psychic, emotional, or mental origin; commonly used to refer to a group of disorders thought to be caused in part or in whole by emotional disturbances but presenting as physiologic derangements" (*Medical Dictionary*).

2. S.I. McMillen, *None of These Diseases* (Old Tappan, N.J.: Fleming H. Revell Co., 1963); H. Selye, *The Stress of Life* (New York: McGraw-Hill Book Co., 1956); O. Tanner, *Human Behavior: Stress* (Alexandria, Va.: Time-Life Books, 1976); S. Wolf and H. Goodell, eds., *Harold G. Wolff's Stress and Disease,* 2nd ed. (Springfield, Ill.: C.C. Thomas, 1968).

3. E. Palmore, "Predicting Longevity: A Follow-up Controlling for Age," *Gerontologist* 9 (1969): 247-50.

tian church. It was revived in the seventeenth century by the philosopher, René Descartes. This fragmentation of man into two supposedly separate substances has led many to despise the body and value the "soul" or to imagine that bodily health could coexist with spiritual confusion. It has blinded us to the fact that life is indivisibly one, that health means what its family of words suggests: *health, whole, wholesome, hale, holy*. Thus, it is absurd to approach the subject of health piecemeal. This fragmentation of man is itself a disease.

> This separation of the soul from the body and from the world is no disease of the fringe, no aberration, but a fracture that runs through the mentality of institutional religion like a geologic fault. And this rift in the mentality of religion continues to characterize the modern mind, no matter how secular or worldly it becomes.[4]

So we do not leave physical health in considering mental health. We cannot talk about this aspect of life in isolation. Since *mind* is only another word for *heart,* we must now get to the heart of the whole subject of human well-being — and this is right mental attitude.

The Search for a Basis of Self-Respect

The word *attitude* may be loosely used to describe how we think and feel about things. But it primarily refers to the way we believe. Our attitude is the way we see and value things at the deepest level of our existence. Let us suppose we believe we are worthless and our lives have no value or meaning. That belief is our attitude. Our belief or attitude will determine our actions, good or bad. If we believe we are worthless, we will treat ourselves as worthless. And it is a law that we will treat others and the environment the same way. A great scholar once said, "A man's view of himself determines his life." For this reason we must first consider our attitude toward ourselves.

---

4. W. Berry, *The Unsettling of America: Culture and Agriculture* (San Francisco: Sierra Club Books, 1977), pp. 108-9.

Do we respect ourselves? Do we believe we are important? Do we have a sense of self-worth? Do we believe our lives have meaning, significance and value?

With a right attitude our answer will be "Yes" to these questions. But right attitude means more than that. It means to have a secure *basis* for saying "Yes." It is one thing to base a sense of self-worth on illusion, and quite another thing to base it on reality. If it is based on illusion, the stresses, frustrations or tragedies of life will cause the vital structure of existence to collapse.

So we must now ask the crucial question, "On what basis do we respect and accept ourselves? On what basis do we believe our lives have meaning, significance and value?" We are really asking, "What is the foundation of our existence and what are we living for?" Health is impossible without a right answer to these questions.

All of us have a self-value system. From childhood on we unconsciously acquire self-value from our parents and peers. We don't have to be very observant to see that the pretty girl gets the attention, the smart boy gets the pats on the back, "Muscles" gets the prizes, and having the right-colored skin helps in some places too.

The value system reflected in these practices is wholly superficial. Is it any wonder that many children nurse the wounds of inferiority, shame and self-reproach because they are not pretty or clever or strong? But the privileged few at the top of the pile of broken bodies are not so privileged after all. They, more than any others, accept this phony value system. The things on which they build their lives soon fade. When they fall from the pile, they are left shattered, empty and haunted with memories.

If our self-value system is tied to beauty, what happens if we become disfigured or grow old and wrinkled? Furthermore, if we accept ourselves on such superficial grounds, we will only accept and respect beautiful people. The same thing applies to physical prowess, intelligence or success. All these can fade or fail us, sometimes with devastating suddenness.

Basing our sense of self-worth, meaning and significance on what we are in ourselves greatly increases our stress. We live in fear of failure. Because we are so psychologically committed to our own achievement and success, we cannot avoid being competitive in our relationship with others. It is a law that when we define the terms on which we accept ourselves, we also define the terms on which we accept others.

Our self-image and self-value, therefore, cannot be securely based on anything we are in ourselves. And for the benefit of the religious reader we add, this includes the religious, pious and Spirit-filled self. Why is it that many religious people are so psychologically lacking in love that they cannot respect and accept those outside their own holy city? The answer should be evident. All attempts to find intrinsic value within ourselves on which to base our self-worth are narcissism, hedonism and subjectivism,[5] and must lead to disintegration of the personality.

Earlier we said that we have various faculties like sight, hearing, speech, mobility, sexuality, intelligence and affections. But none of these constitutes man. They have meaning, value and significance only in the setting of our relationships. Human life is not only defined relationally but valued relationally. We have value only because we are related to something outside ourselves.

This is the most crucial point we have reached in our pursuit of life. So let us dwell here until the point is crystal clear. A thing does not have to have intrinsic worth to be valuable. Most things men fight and die for have only relational value. Diamonds, for instance, are but little pieces of compressed carbon. If people did not esteem them as valuable, they would not be valuable. Neither is the value of gold determined by its usefulness. Its value is determined by what people think of it. Paper dollars are not valuable in themselves. Their value is related to gold, to national productivity or to some other thing.

Let us take the case of a child who is handicapped and severely retarded. He is no less precious in the eyes of his loving parents. They value him, not because of what he is, but regardless of what he is. His preciousness is in the hearts of his parents. Value is relational.

---

5. *"narcissism* . . . self-love; excessive interest in one's own appearance, comfort, importance, abilities, etc."; *"hedonism* . . . the self-indulgent pursuit of pleasure as a way of life";*"subjectivism* . . . an ethical theory holding that personal attitudes and feelings are the sole determinants of moral and aesthetic values" *(Webster's New World Dictionary of the American Language,* 2nd college ed.).

But what is the relationship that gives ultimate value and meaning to life? This is the most important question. Everywhere people are searching for meaning. Frankl, the well-known psychiatrist and author, reports that more than half of those who pass through psychiatric clinics suffer from noogenic neurosis — a condition arising from complete emptiness and lack of meaning in personal existence.[6]

Although life is cast in a variety of relationships, some ultimate relationship, some ultimate reference point, is fundamental to human existence. Life without a supreme relationship, a commitment to a supreme good, an ultimate reference point, is going nowhere and has no real meaning or significance. A sailor in the middle of the Pacific on a dark night cannot get a compass reading off his own navel. To find his heading he must relate himself to a fixed reference point like the North Star or the Southern Cross. Life without a fixed reference point has no stability, no direction, and makes no sense.

What are the options?

One person may base his self-worth on his relationship with the environment. He measures his worth by a sailboat, color television, holiday cottage, luxury bathtub and Persian rugs. We call this value system materialism. Since he values himself by things, he reduces his value to the level of a thing. If he is asked, "How much are you worth?" he immediately counts his things. If he hasn't ruined his "health" to get them, he is ready to jeopardize his "health" to keep them. If he can't hold on to those things which support his self-esteem, he is utterly devastated. Because he has reduced himself to the value of things, he reduces others to the value of things. People become things to be used and exploited as if they were impersonal assets or liabilities. The materialist dehumanizes not only himself but others.

Another person may base his sense of ultimate worth on his relationship with others — family, friends or society. We call this value system socialism. But if he bases his ultimate worth on his relationship to a particular person, upon whom does this other person base his ultimate worth? The dedicated socialist admits that a person has no value in isolation. He contends that society has value and therefore a person derives value from his relationship to society. But society is only a collection of people. A collection of zeros added or multiplied together can only equal zero. If this value system is carried to its logical end, the individual is worth nothing — and is often treated as nothing.

Let us suppose a person finds nothing within himself on which to base his self-worth. So he tries to derive status from his relationship with others — some person more famous than he, some club, church or other group of people. In this relationship he may "unselfishly" serve, but only that he may extract status for himself.

> The more a man feels he really is nobody, the more he craves this esteem in the eyes of others. Even man's unselfish acts are really designed to prove that he is "better" than other, more egotistical souls. In love, this attempt to make oneself something at the expense of others is most insidious.
>
> In a world without meaning, where man is nothing, love can be nothing else but this desire to degrade another. Love cannot be genuine giving, sharing and communion, if man possesses nothing of value to give or to share. If a man cannot stand himself, he will certainly not reverence his lover. Each lover will strive pitifully to extract from his lover a recognition, a proof that he is somebody.[7]

A man who bases his self-value system on himself, others or the environment dehumanizes himself. Instead of finding self-respect, he destroys it. Although his relationship to the environment, others and himself is essential to humanness, he is still incomplete. All his relationships in this world need to be grounded in an ultimate reality, in something intrinsically good. Man does not have intrinsic value, individually or collectively. For one thing he dies. And that which ends in death has no intrinsic value.

The truth is that man is related to God, the Supreme Creator, the personal God who made man in His own image and put him on

---

7. C.S. Evans, *Despair: A Moment or a Way of Life?* (Downers Grove, Ill.: Inter-Varsity Press, 1971), p. 61.

this earth (Genesis 1:26, 27). Unless a man sees himself as related to God, he can never be whole. Above everything else, this is what it means to be human. Man cannot deny this most fundamental fact of his humanness without dehumanizing himself. Here is the relationship which undergirds all other relationships. For man to deny his relationship to God is as foolish as denying his relationship to others or to the environment.

If man is not related to God, he has no value and life has no meaning. If God is dead, man also is dead. At most, he becomes merely a configuration of molecules. Freedom is an illusion. He is both an accidental product and victim of circumstances. Like an organ stop, he cannot act but only react. If there is no God, death says, "Finish." Life is then a journey toward nothing. And that which ends in nothing is worth nothing. Death rises up to crush him like a discarded cigarette butt under the heel of a meaningless universe. Is it indeed the destiny of this creature, with such profound yearning for meaning, to vanish like a bubble?

That is not all. Without God there is no basis to affirm a moral order, no reason to say that one action is right and another wrong. "If there is no God, then everything is permitted," the novelist Fyodor Dostoevski has one of his characters say.[8] If death ends all, then in the final analysis it doesn't make any difference whether I wring my neighbor's neck or shake his hand. And it doesn't make any ultimate difference whether I look after my life or recklessly snuff it out in a riot of indulgence.

"Much of the sickness in our community today is that in killing God, we have found nothing with which to replace Him."[9] The whole moral value system of Western civilization was once built on belief in a Supreme Being. Even unbelievers subscribed to the absolute values derived from a theistic world view. But civilization has run the gamut from deism to naturalism, from naturalism to nihilism, and from nihilism to despair. Despair means life lived without significance or meaning. Man has made for himself a lonely universe. He has a void in his heart like the void in the heart of a child whose father has died.

The Bible is God's word to man. It makes no effort to prove that

---

8. F. Dostoevski, *The Brothers Karamazov* (Baltimore: Penguin Books, 1968), p. 733.

9. G. I. Tewfik, "Community Psychiatry," *Medical Journal of Australia* 1 (1974): 495-98.

man is a creature of God. It simply tells us that our own conscience is the indestructible consciousness that we are related to
God. God's word speaks to that consciousness — that universal,
inward sense that God is. It is this awareness of God which gives
us the awareness of ourselves — self-consciousness. We can stand
"outside" ourselves in self-reflection and judge ourselves. This is
what it means to be a person. This is a mysterious and unique
feature of human existence. We are like this only because we have
been made in God's image and have an ineradicable awareness of
God. He is a person, and our personhood is grounded in the
personhood of God.

Thus, man is related to God, and only in the light of this
relationship can man be truly human or healthy or whole. Here is
where his value is based. Here is where his neighbor's value is
based. And here is where the value of the environment is based.
Man's sense of self-respect and self-worth can only be grounded in
his relationship to God.

5

The Conditions for Life

We saw that the ten laws of life would lead us to the mountain peak where the treasure called life is hidden. On reaching right mental attitude, however, we found we hadn't attained the peak at all. It was only a plateau. Now we see that the summit is still far beyond. But having come this far without too much difficulty, let us take courage and press on.

As we continue, we must keep in mind what we have already learned about the life of wholeness or total health:

1. Life is being truly human. This means being rightly related to the environment, to others and to ourselves.

2. All relationships are defined and governed by law. The laws of human existence are unalterable, and health means being in harmony with them.

3. Right mental attitude is the law which undergirds all others in human existence. Wholeness of life is having a right attitude to ourselves, to others and to the environment. It begins with a right attitude to ourselves.

4. The only solid basis for self-respect and belief in our own self-value is the fact that we are related to God. Apart from God

there is no basis for self-respect or for the value of anything.

This unexpected confrontation with God may have caught some by surprise. "How did 'God talk' get into this?" But did anyone seriously think we could traverse the path to total life and detour around spiritual health? Impossible! Some believe life has a spiritual dimension but imagine it can be isolated from the rest of life. They think they can separate body from soul. But life is one. Health is wholeness. And those who keep spiritual health in a room by itself can never be fully healthy.

Since we are human, we are related to God as much as to our bodies. There was a time when society treated sickness as if man were only a physicochemical machine. Today we know better. We know that mental processes profoundly influence a person's well-being. Man's well-being is inseparable from spiritual health. If a man is not whole, he is not healthy.

We are now ready to state the principle of right mental attitude. A right attitude to ourselves, to others and to the environment depends on a right attitude to God. Right attitude means to believe He is supremely worthy, that He alone possesses supreme worth. From this word *worth* we derive the word *worship*. Having a right attitude to God therefore means worshiping Him (giving Him worth) as He ought to be worshiped — from the deepest level of our existence.

If we do not give God His worth, we will give supreme worth (worship) to something else. This is an inescapable law of existence. We are physical-social-spiritual beings. We are driven to find an object of worship just as we are driven to food and companions. Without good food we will substitute bad food. Without good company we will settle for bad. We must give supreme worth to something. If we do not give it to God, we can only give it to ourselves, to others or to things. There are no other options.

The Worship of Self

Worshiping ourselves, ascribing supreme worth to ourselves, is a bad attitude toward ourselves. It is selfish, egocentric, narcissistic. It makes us megalomaniacs.[1] It prevents us from being truly human, for we cannot be human as long as we play God. Because it is impossible to freely admit our failures, we parade in a flimsy masquerade, putting up a ridiculous front to give an illusion of our own worth. We can never face the rude truth about ourselves. We can never have rest. Making self the object of worship inevitably leads to self-hate, self-contempt and the disintegration of the personality. "Whoever exalts himself will be humbled" (Matthew 23:12).[2]

The Worship of Others

Let us suppose, then, that we worship a person or a group of persons such as the party or the church. This attitude toward others can only dehumanize, degrade and destroy both them and us. Let us take the case of a "perfect" daughter doted on by worshipful parents. Without warning she tries to take her life. Her parents are shocked, for this seems entirely out of keeping with the way their child has always behaved. Unfortunately, they had placed her on such a pedestal that she hated herself for not being what she was supposed to be. The attitude of her parents helped destroy her.

An attitude of worshiping a person may give him such power that he is corrupted by it. Hitler was destroyed by the wrong attitude of those who put him in power. He received a torrent of worship, and the atrocities which marked his career illustrate what can happen to a man who is worshiped. "Power corrupts, and absolute power corrupts absolutely." When a man or group of men

---

1. A megalomaniac is a person with "a mental disorder characterized by delusions of grandeur, wealth, power, etc.," by "a passion for, or for doing, big things," with "a tendency to exaggerate" (Webster's Dictionary).

2. Unless otherwise noted, Old Testament references are from the Revised Standard Version and New Testament references are from the New International Version.

are placed where God should be, they become beasts which destroy both themselves and others.[3]

The only One able to cope with absolute power is the One who had it all but willingly laid it aside to stoop and wash the feet of men quarreling over who should be the greatest. The greatest of all proved Himself the meekest and lowliest of all. To Him alone is it right and safe to ascribe glory, might, dominion and power for ever and ever!

The Worship of Things

What happens if we give supreme worth to the material order? There is no need to guess. By our supreme devotion to materialism we are despoiling and destroying our environment. The deification of science and material progress by modern man has led to the rape and pollution of nature on the one hand, and to the dehumanization of man on the other.

A right attitude to ourselves, to others and to the environment, therefore, is not possible unless we give God His worth.

Giving God His Worth

What does it mean to give supreme worth to God? We have seen that all relationships are defined by law. Our relationship to God is no exception. There are four principles of right worship. Being rightly related to God means believing that He alone is supremely worthy of our absolute loyalty, submission, reverence and devotion.

1. *Loyalty.* As our Supreme Good, He alone is worthy of our unqualified loyalty. He is to come first in everything and is to be trusted as our supreme consolation and support.

2. *Submission.* He alone is worthy of our unqualified submission. Instead of trying to manipulate Him or make Him like

---

3. Read about this in Daniel 7 and Revelation 13.

ourselves, we must submit to Him, allowing Him to make us like Himself.

3. *Reverence.* He is supremely worthy of our deepest admiration and respect because He is goodness, truth and beauty personified.

4. *Devotion.* As Creator of all things, He is worthy of the devotion of all our time.

These four principles are summarized in one word: love. Giving supreme worth to God means obeying the greatest commandment of the Bible: "Love the Lord your God with all your heart, and with all your soul, with all your mind and with all your strength" (Mark 12:30). There can be no reservation, nothing kept back. To love means to go out of oneself to another. It means wholly forgetting oneself in concern for the other. This is important. We must see that we cannot find self-worth by extracting it from our relationship to God any more than we can extract self-worth from people or things. A good marriage relationship, for instance, cannot exist when each party uses the other to establish his or her own value.

Love is to forget oneself for the other. He who tries to find his life loses it. But he who loses his life to God finds it. How does he find it? Instead of defining his own value, he lets God define it. He finds that God puts a far higher value upon him than the miserable value he puts on himself. God does not love him because of his value, but he is valuable because God loves him. This is relational value. It exists wholly in the eye of the Beholder. This value is beyond computation because he is precious in the eyes of an infinitely valuable Being. This is the only way to find true self-respect — at once both great and humbling.

Thus, when man gives supreme worth to God, he finds worth for himself. In giving glory to God he finds dignity for himself. He is truly human because he lets God be God.

Right Attitude to Others

Right attitude to God, believing that He is supremely worthy, leads to a right attitude to ourselves — believing that we are worthy of self-respect. This becomes the basis for our right attitude to others. We can then believe they too are related to God and should be treated with dignity and respect. God defines the value of every human being. When we believe this, we will go out of ourselves to secure their best good. This kind of love is enjoined upon us in the golden rule, "Do unto others as you would have them do unto you."

This unconditional respect for man is social health. We cannot be whole without it. The way we relate to people has a profound influence even on our physical health. In the words of the poet W. H. Auden, "We must love one another or die."[4]

We may define social health with six principles: respect for human authority, respect for human life, respect for human sexuality, respect for human rights, respect for human reputation and respect for the human condition. Let us briefly explore each principle.

1. *Respect for Human Authority.* Human society cannot exist without structures of authority invested in such persons as parents, teachers, judges and state ministers. The only person who is really free is the person who can gladly submit to an authority higher than himself. No human authority, of course, is absolute. Therefore we should never give any man or human institution the unconditional loyalty which belongs only to God.

Those in authority should unconditionally respect the persons subject to them and by just governance provide for their maximum security and individual responsibility. In the parent-child relationship the child should always know that his acceptance is certain. He should feel he is accepted whether he succeeds or fails. Every child needs discipline and may sometimes need punishment. But he should never be led to think this is an act of rejection. He must never feel he has to "buy" his parents' acceptance with a particular kind of behavior.

2. *Respect for Human Life.* Since man has been placed in a special relationship to God, loved by an infinitely loving Being, there should be reverence for all human life. This means refrain-

---

4. Quoted in "Loneliness Can Kill You," *Time,* 5 Sept. 1977, p. 45.

ing from anything which deprives others of their legitimate right to full enjoyment of life. It also means promoting the maximum quality of life for everyone. This has vast implications. We could well reflect on the pollution of air, water, soil and cities in the light of respect for human life.

3. *Respect for Human Sexuality.* It was God who created the basic relationships of human existence. He made man male and female (Genesis 1:27, 28). The force of this simple fact must not escape us. Man is male plus female. Male alone is not a whole man. Neither is female. Man is a being of community. This is not an appendage of human existence. It *is* human existence. The sexual distinction was God's idea, and we can therefore accept it as a good idea. By this He would teach us that wholeness cannot be found in competition or in isolation. Wholeness is only found in coming together, in caring and sharing, in forgetting oneself, in going out of oneself to another. Marriage is the institution of divine arrangement which symbolizes this and therefore is to be celebrated by the community. It is also designed to illustrate the sacred union between God and man. Just as man cannot be truly human except in community, so he cannot be truly human except in union with God.

Marriage can invest life with some of its deepest emotions and highest joys. Its consummation was designed to be intensely pleasurable, to symbolize that the greatest satisfaction in life is not found in being alone but in giving one's self for the other. In this, marriage expresses the essence of what it means to be truly human.

It cannot be said, therefore, that human sexuality is unimportant. It is important. Every member of the race is labeled sexually at birth. Life would be dull if not impossible without the male/female distinction. This distinction has inspired much of man's best music, literature, art and noble enterprises. It has brought out some of the best qualities in the human spirit.

This does not mean that all must be married to participate in wholeness. But it does mean that all must participate in supporting the institution of marriage as God has defined it and that all must participate in the principle of self-giving, which marriage is meant to teach. Marriage belongs to the whole community. A man's covenant union with one woman is not just a contract with one, but it is a contract with the community. Faithfulness in his covenant with one is faithfulness in his covenant with all.

As we already know, health belongs to a family of words: *health, whole, wholesome, hale, holy*. When sexuality is isolated from the rest of life and becomes a preoccupation in itself, it is emptied of all meaning. Separated from the wholeness of human existence, it is autonomous, frivolous and destructive even of itself. When sex is reduced to a mere physical dimension, it can become as boring as barnyard physiology.

Man's deepest feelings and beliefs need to be expressed in appropriate physical actions or symbols. We see this in such things as patriotism, religious convictions and fraternal group interests. We give flowers, send cards and make other appropriate gestures to express our feelings. Our lives are enriched by actions which symbolize feelings and beliefs too deep to express any other way.

But the mere imitation of these signs is empty, disrespectful or even sacrilegious. Thus, sexual encounter has legitimate meaning and satisfying potential only in the total union of male and female, only where there is unconditional commitment and a sense of consequence and responsibility. The sexually promiscuous are not to be censured for "going all the way" but for *not* going all the way. The Casanova who wanders from one amorous relationship to another is to be pitied. He has destroyed his capacity for wholeness in any relationship. Human sexuality clearly illustrates that human life cannot be fragmented without destroying its meaning.

Human consciousness has always identified the distortion of human sexuality with impurity. That is, human sexuality is adulterated; hence the word *adultery*. Our sexuality becomes impure if:

a. It does not express God's undeviating faithfulness to man, and man's obligation of undeviating faithfulness to God.

b. It does not express wholeness by the union of two opposites which were designed by God to complement — to make whole, to complete — each other.

c. It does not express going out of oneself for the benefit of the other.

d. It does not express total, permanent and unconditional self-giving.

4. *Respect for Human Rights.* Man is a person because he is made in the image of God. He possesses individuality. He has power to think and to do. He has creativity, inventiveness and imagination. Personhood also means that he has options. He has the faculty of self-determination. He is not a mere organ stop who can only react to his environment. He has the capacity to act on his environment.

A right attitude toward others will not dehumanize them by robbing them of their God-given rights. Not only will it protect their right to decide how they should use their creativity and its products, but it will also protect their rights of privacy, freedom of speech and freedom of religion.

5. *Respect for Human Reputation.* No principle of social health is violated so frequently as this. With a right attitude toward others we will not indulge in slander, gossip or misrepresentation. When our self-respect is based upon the value God gives us, we won't pull others down to lift ourselves up.

If our neighbor's life is at stake or if his house is on fire, we naturally go to his aid. But how few of us defend his character when he is misrepresented!

> They are slaves who fear to speak
> For the fallen and the weak;
> They are slaves who will not choose
> Hatred, scoffing, and abuse,
> Rather than in silence shrink
> From the truth they needs must think;
> They are slaves who dare not be
> In the right with two or three.[5]

6. *Respect for the Human Condition.* God has given man his essential relationships. By these He has defined what it means to

---

5. J.R. Lowell, "Stanzas for Freedom," *The Great Quotations,* comp. G. Seldes (New York: Lyle Stuart, 1966), p. 442.

be truly human. Made in God's image, man is related to God. Created male and female, he is related to the community. Given a physical body, he is related to the material world. He has been placed in the world to rule it and to use it responsibly for his own pleasure and for God's praise. Man has a natural affinity for his material environment, yet he is at the same time above it. He is not God and he is not a thing. He is, as it were, set between heaven and earth, for he is under God and over the world. Ruled by God, he in turn is to rule the world as God's vicegerent. Man is defined by these God-given relationships.

A right attitude demands that we respect the human condition and be content with what the Creator has given us to be. It means being content with our finitude, not trying to be God. God has defined human value, and that value is great because we are related to and loved by a great God. We cannot find this great value in ourselves. We never can and never will. It is a relational value. In this we should be content, not coveting the kind of value God has — intrinsic, inherent, ontological value.[6] He has defined the boundaries of human existence by laws as fixed as the stars in their courses. We must be content to live within the jurisdiction of law, for that is part of creature existence.

A right attitude means we will be content with our own sexuality and gladly accept the consequent privileges and obligations. We will also be content with our own body, individuality and gifts without wanting to be someone else. We will not be jealous when others prosper, but from the heart will be glad in another's success. We will not secretly rejoice when another stumbles or fails.

When we are content with the dignity and self-worth God has given us, we can also have a right attitude to the environment. We will not try to acquire status and dignity for ourselves by the reckless exploitation of nature. Neither will we deify nature by finding in it our consolation and support. We know that it is God's creation and that it is there as surely as God is there. Therefore we will not mystically think of the material order as a mere illusion to be ignored or transcended. There is beauty, order and

---

6. "You [God] alone are holy" (Revelation 15:4). God "alone is immortal" (1 Timothy 6:16). "No one is good — except God alone" (Mark 10:18).

genuine pleasure in the world. When we are content to be truly human, we will not have a world-denying, world-hating view of life. It is given us to laugh and play as well as to weep and work. God's world is to be used and enjoyed in an attitude of celebration.

The Law of Life

In outlining what it means to have a right mental attitude, we have simply stated the principles of the Ten Commandments. This is the greatest law ever given. It is the basis of the Judeo-Christian ethic, the foundation of the moral code of Western civilization. Though many have tried to tamper with it and have rained their blows upon it, it is an anvil which has worn out many hammers. Toward God it enjoins supreme love, manifested in absolute

> Loyalty
> Submission
> Reverence
> Devotion

Toward man it enjoins impartial love, manifested in respect for human

> Authority
> Life
> Sexuality
> Rights
> Reputation
> Condition

This is a description of right mental attitude. Indeed, it is a succinct summary of our whole duty. These commandments contain ten principles which undergird and embrace all human existence. They define what it means to be in right relationship to God, to ourselves, to others and to the environment. Spiritual, social and physical health are all included. This law defines what it means to be truly human. It is a whole law for a whole, wholesome, holy, healthy man.

The law says, "Do this and you will live." "The man who does these things [the commandments] will live by them" (Luke 10:28;

Romans 10:5). Jesus Himself said, "If you want to enter life, obey the commandments" (Matthew 19:17). Saint Paul declared, "It is those who obey the law who will be declared righteous" (Romans 2:13).

This law extends to the thoughts and intents of the heart as well as to the outward actions (Matthew 5:21-28; Romans 7:7). Since it is a perfect law, it must be kept in every part or it is not kept at all (James 2:10). It is so just and reasonable that no one can have any legitimate excuse for not doing it. He who fails to carry it out — every jot and tittle of it — falls under its curse (Galatians 3:10). He deserves to die (Romans 6:23).

6

The Impossibility of Life

In our pursuit of life we have found that right mental attitude will present some hard climbing. We understand what we ought to do. That is plain enough. The problem is doing it. The mountain now rises before us in terrifying grandeur. It is a sheer cliff thousands of feet high, and on it are the ten steps to right mental attitude. Each must be executed perfectly. One slip means death. Although a dark cloud now obscures the mountain, flashes of lightning occasionally reveal the glorious outline of the summit we seek.

Cutting across the face of this great mountain is another path. It gives us a ray of hope so we move ahead, pressing close to the great rock wall, not daring to look below. Suddenly the path ends at the brink of a huge abyss. Lightning illuminates the mighty chasm. Strewn on the rocks below are the bones of those who have tried to scale this mountain for the treasure called life. As we pause in mingled awe and terror, we grasp the meaning of the abyss.

Alienation

Because we have been pursuing life and health, we have not

talked about disease. We have learned that health is being rightly related to all the connections of human existence. It is being in harmony with the earth, with the community of people and with ourselves. We will now look briefly—only briefly—at unhealth. It is the opposite of fitting comfortably into all the relationships of human existence. Unhealth is a fracture, a disruption and disintegration of those relationships which define what it means to be truly human. In one word, unhealth is alienation.

We choose the word *alienation* because it aptly describes the seat of human disease and because it has become prominent in the language of ecologists, philosophers, sociologists and even revolutionaries. Ecologists see man estranged from his identity with the earth. Technological, urbanized man is so estranged from the earth that to him it is just an empty environment. He has lost his feeling for nature and does not see himself as part of it. He has lost his roots in the earth. The women's liberation movement has highlighted a dimension of social alienation. Civil-rights crusaders have been making war on racial alienation. Sociologists have been grappling with the problem of how modern technology and specialization have alienated man from the meaning which comes from pride and satisfaction in work. Churches are in the midst of upheaval as they attempt to overcome the alienation of the clergy from the laity. Dedicated statesmen are wrestling with the problem of national and international alienation.

Even Marx spoke about the human situation in terms of alienation. He saw man alienated by economic forces, and he highlighted the tensions of the class struggle. Like most modern crusaders against alienation, Marx blamed it on the system. "Change the system!" shout the protest marchers. They think evil springs from the environment. But this blind spot highlights how deep-seated the alienation really is. If the problem does spring from the system, if the system alone is the source of evil, man has lost his individuality. He is only a thing conditioned by circumstances. He has no self-determinative personality. He cannot act but only react. This philosophy shows that man is so alienated at the very center of his existence that he can see himself as a depersonalized *thing*. He can regard himself as thoroughly conditioned by circumstances outside himself.

We must cease superficial diagnoses and go to the heart of the human disease called alienation. Man is alienated from himself, and all alienation between neighbors, between the sexes, between man and the earth springs from the alienation of man from himself. So let us now try to understand self-alienation.

We have already pointed out that man has a relationship with himself. He is not only conscious, but self-conscious and self-reflective. He is able to stand "outside" himself, to reflect on himself and judge his own behavior. Animals cannot do that. Only man does it. This is what it means to be a person.

As we stand apart and reflect on ourselves, we see the self in two different ways. We see the self as we would like it to be — how we feel it ought to be. We also see the self as it actually is. These two views of the self are not always identical. When there is a gap between what we believe we ought to be and what we actually are, we are torn apart and fragmented. If we could forget what we ought to be and just identify with what we are, we would not experience tension. But we are not able to do that. And if the tension becomes too great, we have real problems.

Consider a simple illustration. You feel you should do something worthwhile with your life, serving and loving others unconditionally instead of selfishly living for yourself. You may even set out to be a do-gooder. But there are moments of reflection and self-illumination when you see you are still unbelievably self-seeking. In helping others you are only trying to prove you are something. The self you can alone accept as worthy is not the self you are. At the center of your existence you are torn apart. You condemn and reject yourself. Hence the self-alienation.

We are not talking about a phenomenon which only happens to some people. Every person experiences this to a greater or lesser degree. Who has not realized that he has not done what his inmost being tells him he ought to have done? Who has not spoken words or felt certain feelings that he later wished he had not said or felt? Where is the man who always lives up to his own ideal of what he ought to be? Where is the person who can say, "I am all that I ought to be"? Anyone who does say this is so alienated from himself that his real personality has been destroyed.

When we see that the self is not what it ought to be, we pass judgment upon it. We reject it. This is self-rejection, and with it we experience inferiority, self-shame and self-hate. The severity of this alienation from ourselves can vary in intensity, depending on the mechanisms we use to deal with it.

What we have described is the operation of the human conscience. As the body points us unmistakably to our identification
with the physical order, as sexuality points us unmistakably to
our identity with the social order, so conscience points us unmistakably to our relationship with the spiritual order. Conscience is
the indestructible conviction that we are creatures of God, before
whom we are responsible for our deeds. We might just as well
deny the reality of our own body or sexuality as to deny the reality
of our own conscience.

Whenever by the action of the conscience we pass judgment
against the self, we are alienated from ourselves. Every time we
pretend to be what we are really not, we prove that alienation
exists. We show that we despise our true selves. Every time we
"create an image," we reveal the alienation of self-rejection. Why
do we so often make a mask of the self which is not the true self?
Isn't it because we are ashamed of the true self?

The most subtle self-destructive acting is religious acting.
Jesus called the religious teachers of His day hypocrites. Many of
them were good, moral men. They even had a code which said that
hypocrisy was one of the four worst sins. The word for *hypocrisy* in
the New Testament stories comes from a word which means to be
an actor. In trying to be pious the Pharisees were forced to act
what they really were not. On the outside they were like nice
white tombstones, laudable examples of good citizens. But inside
they were like rotting bones. It was a front so clever and ingenious
that it not only fooled others, it fooled themselves.

There is no end to these ingenious masks we make to hide
ourselves not only from others but from ourselves. Superficial
masks please some people — flashy cars, swanky homes, profes-
sional degrees, titles, membership in elitist clubs. A person may
use these things to advertise, "I'm important," "I've got status,"
"I'm worthy of acceptance."

But then in the silence of the soul the conscience speaks: "You
are a mean, self-seeking, no-good wretch."

"What? Oh no, it can't be. It's a bad dream. Do I have to accept
that? It must be the verdict of an idle brain."

There is nothing like distraction to silence the voice of conscience — this relentless moral judge who points a bony finger at
us every time we are caught in a moment of self-reflection. So we
are driven to become a workaholic. Or perhaps a foodaholic or an

alcoholic or a drugaholic. These are all signs of gnawing, growing alienation.

We are talking about the *sense* of guilt.[1] Guilt is the world's greatest health problem. It contributes to physical disease, chronic depression, worry, fear (especially fear of death), unhappiness, bitterness, remorse, social tension and, of course, self-rejection, self-contempt, self-shame and thus self-hate —*alienation*.

Self-alienation fractures the wholeness (health) of human life. It has a profound influence on man's philosophical assumptions, on his thinking about himself. He alienates body from soul and thinks of himself as two instead of one. He isolates sexuality from the wholeness of life so that it becomes nothing but an unwholesome physical encounter.

Man's self-alienation alienates him from other people. The one who cannot accept and love himself cannot love anyone else. Having nothing to give others, he can only use others to extract worth for himself. Other people are his competitors in the stampede for status, power or attention. He may even look upon nature as hostile, as something to be plundered. Or he may try to find some fusion with nature by projecting upon it the qualities of his own personality.

We sometimes meet "brave" souls who can say nonchalantly, "Guilt is never a problem in my life. It never bothers me." There are three explanations for this:

1. They are perfect. They can look the law in the eye. They measure up in everything. We can only sympathize with their struggle to live with the rest of us imperfect mortals.

2. They are psychopathic and have a deadened conscience — from childhood training which left them morally shriveled, from continually violating their conscience or from serious brain damage. A psychopath is sick and dangerous, not to be trusted.

---

1. The *sense* of guilt is not altogether the same as *actual* guilt. Actual guilt is objective. It refers to a person's *standing* in relation to the moral law — the "ought." On the other hand, the sense of guilt refers to a person's *awareness* of how he stands in relation to the "ought."

3. They are probably neither perfect nor psychopathic. They unconsciously use mental mechanisms — such as compensation, projection, rationalization, reaction-formation, regression, repression and transference — to resolve their guilt.[2] They have become so expert at this that they do not understand their own behavior.

When such physical and mental mechanisms are pointed out, many exclaim, "Oh yes, that's just like me! I do that all the time!" Then it dawns on them that much of their behavior is motivated by guilt and by attempts to avoid it. Some then ask, "Wouldn't it be better to remain ignorant of what we are doing?" Not if we want to be truly human. Besides, the unexamined life is not worth living.

None of these mechanisms gets rid of alienation and guilt. These "cures" only perpetuate the disease. They destroy the personality and increase the guilt. The whole process thus becomes a vicious merry-go-round.

We cannot understand the gravity of self-alienation, however, until we consider man's more serious attempts to bridge the chasm at the center of his existence. These attempts are on the spiritual plane. They are attempts either to keep the law or to get rid of the law.

---

2. "*compensation* . . . In psychoanalysis, the mechanism by which an approved character trait is put forward to conceal from the ego the existence of an opposite trait"; "*projection* . . . a mental mechanism by which a repressed complex is disguised by being regarded as belonging to the external world or to someone else"; "*rationalization* . . . the mental process by which a plausible explanation (justification) is concocted for ideas and beliefs or activities which one wishes to hold or to do; the real motivation being subconscious or at least obscure"; "*reaction-formation* . . . a psychic mechanism by which a person consciously assumes an attitude which is the reverse of, and a substitute for, a repressed antisocial impulse"; "*regression* . . . the turning backward of the libido to an early fixation at infantile levels because of inability to function in terms of reality"; "*repression* . . . In psychiatry, the thrusting back from consciousness into the unconscious sphere of ideas or perceptions of a disagreeable nature"; "*transference* . . . in psychiatry, the shifting of an affect from one person to another or from one idea to another, especially the transference by the patient to the analyst of emotional tones, either of affection or of hostility, based on unconscious identification" *(Medical Dictionary)*.

Keep the Law

Before we can be whole we must close the gap between what the self ought to be and what it actually is. But what makes us feel the compulsion of the "ought"? It is the law. It doesn't have to come to us in the exact form of the Ten Commandments. It may be reflected in the example of big-hearted Bill. Provocation runs off him like water off a duck's back. In a moment of self-reflection we think, "I ought to be like that." We see a diligent fellow student toiling upward while we fritter away precious time and we say, "I ought to quit fooling around." We hear the pledge read at the Lion's Club and respond, "I ought to serve my fellow man as I have pledged." Injustice is done to a church member and we could have a prominent church office if we drifted with the popular current. But a voice says, "You ought to stand up like a man." There is something in us which responds to this "ought," this moral imperative, and it will not be silenced. But when we look at the pure law of God revealed to us in the Bible, the "ought" may no longer be a still, small voice, but a thunderclap waking us to a sense of what we ought to be.

So we set out to bridge the gap between what we ought to be and what we are. We can manage some things in an external way. But we soon find that the law demands purity of motive, unselfishness of purpose, love that loses itself and has no thought of reward. We decide to be unselfish, but the very decision is self-serving. We serve others to find value for ourselves. We try to be humble, but even our trying proves that we are not what we ought to be. We press on in relentless pursuit of what we ought to be, but the path gets steeper, becomes a mountain and finally looms before us as a mighty, impossible cliff where one slip means death. We find another path we think will take us an easier way, but it ends at the brink of an awful chasm.

How wide is the gap between what we ought to be and what we actually are? It is as wide as the gulf between the righteousness of the mighty God and the unrighteousness of feeble man. The whole law must be kept in every part or it is not kept at all. There are no degrees of keeping or of breaking it. True, it says, "Do this and live." But it also says, "One slip and you die." How can a man already fractured and alienated at the center of his existence bridge a gulf as wide as heaven and earth? He might as well think he can touch the stars by climbing a mountain.

So this attempt to find life by keeping the law is a dead-end road. Law only sharpens the "ought," increases the guilt and intensifies the alienation from ourselves — to say nothing of our alienation from God.

Let us now speak frankly about our pursuit of life. When we began this journey, we learned that life is found in compliance with all the unalterable laws of life. There are proper breathing, drinking, eating and securing sufficient sunlight. There are good posture, exercise, rest, moderation and hygiene. Complying with even these physical aspects of life proves difficult. We may run well for a while, but what happens when we fail and are plagued with self-doubt? Besides, there is no end to the things we need to do to have life. As we press on, we move into right mental attitude — compliance with the Ten Commandments. And if we are not yet convinced of our selfish, unreliable and crooked nature, trying to live up to this law soon makes our good resolutions appear as so many South Sea dreams. We feel more frustrated, defeated and alienated than ever. There is also the record of our past failures and the fact that we are what we have been. Unless something can bridge the gulf between what we ought to be and what we are, we will be sorry we ever began our journey toward life and total health.

Get Rid of the Law

Why not get rid of the law if it only sharpens our sense of the "ought" and reveals this gap more keenly? Don't high ethical and moral standards only increase the sense of guilt and misery?

Some "experts" tell us that the only way to resolve the inner conflict is to bring our high and "impractical" ethical ideals down to the level of what we are able to do. "After all, the mayor does it. Even the clergyman does it. In fact, everybody does it. So why feel guilty about it?" Misery loves company.

Roger was in the prime of life. He had a strong body, a lovely wife, four fine children and a prosperous business. But he suffered a moral lapse quite inconsistent with his ideals. Chronic mental depression, the result of guilt, reduced him to a wreck of a man.

He lived on tranquilizers and antidepressants. His psychiatrist told him he could only get rid of his depression by getting rid of his "ridiculously high moral ideals" — the Ten Commandments. But this method of dealing with guilt is like trying to change the temperature by breaking the thermometer.

Getting rid of the law rebounds with an increased burden of guilt. A person cut loose from an absolute standard of right and wrong — the fixed reference point found in the knowledge of God and His unchanging law — has the task of manufacturing his own standards and morals for every situation. This is moral relativism, and it can be very stressful. Uncertainty about what is right and wrong causes real anxiety. Having no fixed moral standards has helped produce "the anxious society."[3] Children brought up without clearly defined boundary lines are insecure. A man is only a grown boy. He may play God Almighty — a very stressful role — but a creature's only security and freedom are under the authority of law.

In spite of himself man is a creature of law. He cannot live without it. His institutions, his important transactions and even the games he plays are related to law. When he wants security for his marriage, his home, his children or his property, he resorts to law. The sense of justice is so indelibly graven in human nature that it cannot be erased. It must be satisfied.

To be human is to have an overriding, indestructible passion to be right in the eyes of the law. This is why we spend so much time and effort justifying ourselves. We cannot be truly human unless we know the dignity of being in the right. This is why we cannot endure guilt. We rationalize our wrong, project our guilt, repress it and compensate for it. Unless we accept ourselves, we remain alienated from ourselves. But we cannot accept ourselves unless we are justified.

We cannot overcome alienation by keeping the law, nor can we overcome it by getting rid of the law. This alienation is our unhealth.

The tensions of guilt and alienation in society are enormous.

---

3. R.W. Roberts, "Living in an Anxious Society," *Australian Family Physician* 1 (1972): 281-85.

Scientific idealism, which promised man so much, has not satisfied his great spiritual hunger. And now, like the breaking forth of an appetite long denied, it drives man in a mad rampage after modern gurus whose "cures" only perpetuate the disease. We can hardly cope with all the new methods of "liberating" people from their "hang-ups" — sensitivity training, self-actualization, crisis of identity, the occult, Tibetan gong therapy, magic, drugs, ad infinitum.

We have considered our alienation from ourselves, from others and from the earth. But if this alienation is a formidable obstacle, what shall we say when we find a much bigger problem? Our alienation from ourselves, others and the earth is but the extension of our alienation from our Creator.

How does God react to this tragic human situation? He can't just slap us on the back and say, "It's all right, Jack. I still love you." It is true that God is love (1 John 4:8), but love for the right implies hate for the wrong. His inexorable law is an expression of His eternal self-consistency. He cannot look with indifference upon that which defiles, degrades and destroys His image in man. His holy nature burns against wrong. As moral Governor of the universe, He cannot take rebellion lightly. Indeed, He would be unjust if He did not treat man with the full justice of His law.

God is a personal Being, more personal than we are since our personhood is only a reflection of His. He is grieved by man's disaffection, and the intensity of His holy anger is in proportion to His love. If He did not love man so much, He would not be so angry.

We say this because some would like to make God into an indulgent parent, complacent and morally indifferent about the son who outrages the family honor. God is not like that. He is wholly righteous. He will see to it that justice is done, that all debts are paid. Thus, as we gaze up from our human predicament, we see that our alienation is infinitely great.

What can we do to get rid of guilt? Absolutely nothing! What good advice can we give to overcome this alienation? Absolutely none! We are inextricably bound to our predicament. All our efforts only increase our guilt. In pursuit of the treasure of life we have reached the final impasse.

Some may now be tempted to turn back, wishing we had never started such a perilous journey. Wouldn't it be better to die back in the land of our cigarettes, sugary flummeries, soft TV chairs and befuddled brains rather than to die on this journey after leaving so many indulgences behind? But now it is so dark that going back would be as fatal as going on.

But just when all hope has fled, a friendly voice rings out above the crash of thunder, "Friends, I have good news. I can get you out of your predicament. Just stand still and listen!"

7

The Verdict of Life

If our journey to the dark abyss called alienation has stalled our pursuit of life, it has accomplished its purpose. We must be so thoroughly chastened that we will cease our efforts and listen to good news — news so unspeakably great that if we will listen we will be lifted high above the mountain summit.

Health is being right in all our relationships. Unhealth is alienation. Healing is found in reconciliation — a task greater than the work of creation. Putting the fractured creation together again is a work only the Almighty can accomplish. Guilt is a God-sized problem. He must handle it. The creation of the world was an exhibition of almighty power and wisdom. But the work of reconciliation is greater. It is a work in which we see the exertion and investment of all the power, wisdom, justice and love of the Creator.

The story of what our heavenly Father has done is the Christian gospel — good news. It is two thousand years old, but it has never lost its thrilling power. As time rolls on, the more amazing it becomes. As the dark shadows of a future without hope deepen with the close of this century, it becomes increasingly clear that the good news is the only solution — a divine solution to reconcile man to his world, to his neighbor, to himself and to his God.

The good news is that God has acted to reconcile the world. He placed Himself in the tragic human situation. In the person of His own Son, by whom He made the world, He became "God with us" (Matthew 1:23) — and not only with us but "for us" (Romans 8:31). It is the nature of love to go out of itself to another, to put itself in the other's shoes, to bear the other's burden. This is what God did in the person of His Christ. He did it because His love called Him that way. He did not do it because the objects of His love were valuable in themselves. The value was in the eye of the Beholder.

The Son of the Eternal God, possessing the nature and glory of the Father, came to this world as the Representative of God. He also became the Representative of man. He became the second Head of the race, as Adam was the first. Thus, He stood before God as mankind.[1] As all the race was represented in the first Adam and fell with the first Adam, so in a mysterious way mankind was also gathered up and represented in Christ, the second Adam.

Born into the world as Jesus of Nazareth, having been conceived by the Holy Spirit, His identity with humanity was complete except that our wretched alienation, which makes us less than truly human, was not in Him. He was truly human although still truly divine. He subjected Himself to the law on our behalf. He was man in God's image, man as man was meant to be. He was the whole, holy, healthy man because He was in right relationship with God, with Himself, with humanity and with the world. He was for us the "ought." He was what we are not.

His identity with us became so complete that He actually identified Himself with our alienation. We see a faint and imperfect illustration of this when a parent suffers vicariously with an injured child. But His identity with us was much closer than any such relationship. Only the divine Creator could mysteriously make Himself so close to all. He bore our alienation as if it were His own. He was born in a stable and laid in a donkey's food box. His earthly parents had to flee with Him into Egypt. And when "He came to that which was His own, . . . His own did not receive Him" (John 1:11).

---

1. See 1 Corinthians 15:45; Romans 5:12-21. Christ is designated as the second or "last Adam." *Adam* means mankind.

He was despised and rejected by men;
    a man of sorrows, and acquainted with grief;
and as one from whom men hide their faces
    He was despised, and we esteemed Him not.

Surely He has borne our griefs
    and carried our sorrows;
yet we esteemed Him stricken,
    smitten by God, and afflicted.
But He was wounded for our transgressions,
    He was bruised for our iniquities;
upon Him was the chastisement that made us whole,
    and with His stripes we are healed.
All we like sheep have gone astray;
    we have turned every one to his own way;
and the Lord has laid on Him
    the iniquity of us all.

He was oppressed, and He was afflicted,
    yet He opened not His mouth;
like a lamb that is led to the slaughter,
    and like a sheep that before its shearers is dumb,
    so He opened not His mouth.
By oppression and judgment He was taken away;
    and as for His generation, who considered
that He was cut off out of the land of the living,
    stricken for the transgression of my people?
And they made His grave with the wicked
    and with a rich man in His death,
although He had done no violence,
    and there was no deceit in His mouth.

Yet it was the will of the Lord to bruise Him;
    He has put Him to grief;
when He makes Himself an offering for sin,
    He shall see His offspring, He shall prolong His days;
the will of the Lord shall prosper in His hand;
    He shall see the fruit of the travail of His soul and
      be satisfied;
by His knowledge shall the Righteous One, My Servant,
    make many to be accounted righteous;
    and He shall bear their iniquities.
Therefore I will divide Him a portion with the great,
    and He shall divide the spoil with the strong;
because He poured out His soul to death,
    and was numbered with the transgressors;
yet He bore the sin of many,
    and made intercession for the transgressors.
                    —Isaiah 53:3-12.

He Was Called to Judgment

God is not only merciful but also terrible in His justice. His law must be reckoned with. Even human experience should tell us that the great laws of life are not only inexorable, never changing, but penal—bringing an inevitable penalty upon the transgressor. God could not look on the sinful human situation with complacency. His very justice and holiness demanded that He take action. And He did — with a justice both uncompromising and terrible.

On that Good Friday—alas, not good for Him, only for us—He arraigned the world in judgment. We were all there in our Head and Representative. God judged Him. And although He was all that we ought to be—for never had one walked the earth so pure and holy — He was condemned, justly condemned in the awful judgment of God. We say justly because God judges man relationally, and this Man stood identified with us. The penalty was not mitigated. There were no special favors. There was nothing pretty or sentimental about Calvary. It was a gruesome, bloody execution.

> Christ died for our sins according to the Scriptures. — 1 Corinthians 15:3.
>
> You see, at just the right time, when we were still powerless, Christ died for the ungodly. . . . God demonstrates His own love for us in this: While we were still sinners, Christ died for us.—Romans 5:6, 8.
>
> God made Him who had no sin to be sin for us, so that in Him we might become the righteousness of God. — 2 Corinthians 5:21.
>
> Christ redeemed us from the curse of the law by becoming a curse for us, for it is written: "Cursed is everyone who is hanged on a tree." — Galatians 3:13.

See this mysterious Victim hung between heaven and earth! As the Judge, He took the place of those who should have been judged. He bore the full brunt of the world's alienation. He bore the curse of nature, represented in a crown of thorns. The sun was darkened. He thirsted for drink. He was rejected by His own people and derided in His dying agonies. But far more terrible than all, He seemed shut out from God and from hope itself. To the depths of His soul He felt the terrors of hell—desperate loneliness and God-forsakenness. From His lips was wrung that awful cry, "My God, My God, why have You forsaken Me?" The black shadows of eternal night without hope of morning tore His great heart and slew Him.

But that is not all. He took unto Himself our alienation that He might reconcile the world unto God. And He did just that (Romans 5:10). All the relationships of human existence were represented at the cross. His feet were pointed to the earth, His arms outstretched to embrace the human family, His holy head bowed to accept the verdict from heaven. By dying He brought God and man and earth together.

> . . . and through Him to reconcile to Himself all things, whether things on earth or things in heaven, by making peace through His blood, shed on the cross.
> Once you were alienated from God and were enemies in your minds because of your evil behavior. But now He has reconciled you by Christ's physical body through death to present you holy in His sight, without blemish and free from accusation. — Colossians 1:20-22.

And that is not all. His righteousness was so mighty that it swallowed up the world's sin, His life so eternally great that it swallowed up death. On the third day He rose from the dead, was seen by many witnesses and then ascended in human flesh into the presence of God as the accepted man. Thus was the race restored to favor with God in the person of its Representative. And in Him who embraces all men, man is whole, holy, healthy. In all this, God has neither been lenient with sin nor short on mercy. If we will believe it, the death of God's Son was our death. "One died for all, and therefore all died" (2 Corinthians 5:14). If we will believe it, His resurrection was our acceptance into divine favor. If we will believe it, God freely forgave us at Calvary at His own expense. Like the true Father that He is, He spared His children but not Himself.

If one should ask how the righteousness of One and the dying of One can be considered the righteousness of many and the death of many, we can simply answer that the gospel says so. But we can also say that since sin and death came into this world by one man, then it is proper for God to remove it by one man (Romans 5:12, 18,

19; 1 Corinthians 15:21). We are afflicted by that individualism of the Western mind which makes us think that each man lives as an island. This is not so. All human life is mysteriously connected. Every day we live by what others do for us. Our parents, our children and our state officials represent us in many things. Life is continually supported by what others do. We prosper or suffer by what others do. And our own influence reaches out to affect many others.

> No man is an island, entire of itself; every man is a piece of the continent, a part of the main. . . . Any man's death diminishes me, because I am involved in mankind; and therefore never send to know for whom the bell tolls; it tolls for thee.[2]

This illustrates how the doing and dying of that One who was righteous can be the doing and dying of the many who are sinners. As one believer has well said, "Mine are Christ's living, doing, and speaking, His suffering and dying, mine as much as if I had lived, done, spoken, suffered, and died as He did."

We Are Now Called to Judgment

Now that God has acted in Christ for the judgment of the whole world, He must bring us to personally participate in it, either to accept what He has done or to refuse it. By the proclamation of this one everlasting gospel God arraigns the inhabitants of the world to judgment. And by their response to what He has graciously done in Christ, each man is judged. And more, each man passes judgment on himself. The final judgment day at the end of the world will only confirm and manifest what the verdict has been — His verdict and ours.

The gospel divides the race into two: those who believe and those who believe not. Those who believe not are judged and condemned (Mark 16:16).

> Anyone who does not believe God has made Him out to be a liar.
> —1 John 5:10.

---

2. J. Donne, *Devotions,* 17, quoted in John Bartlett, *Familiar Quotations,* 13th ed. (Boston: Little, Brown & Co., 1955), p. 218.

> Whoever does not believe stands condemned already because he
> has not believed in the name of God's one and only Son. —John 3:18.

> Whoever puts his faith in the Son has eternal life, but whoever
> rejects the Son will not see that life, for God's wrath remains on
> him. —John 3:36.

On the other hand, those who believe are forgiven. By the
verdict of the divine court they are pronounced justified.

> For all . . . are justified freely by His grace through the redemp-
> tion that came by Christ Jesus. God presented Him as a sacrifice of
> atonement, through faith in His blood. . . . For we maintain that a
> man is justified by faith apart from observing the law. —Romans
> 3:23-25, 28.

> I tell you the truth, whoever hears My word and believes Him
> who sent Me has eternal life and will not be condemned; he has
> crossed over from death to life. —John 5:24.

> For God so loved the world that He gave His one and only Son,
> that whoever believes in Him shall not perish but have everlasting
> life. —John 3:16.

Two men hear the gospel and are thereby brought to judgment.
One is a man of many splendid virtues. He has lived well before
men and is honored in the community. He does not do bad as men
count badness. In fact, his life is devoted to good as men count
goodness. But he does not believe the gospel. He is condemned.
The verdict is just because at the deepest level of existence he is
an alienated sinner and proves it by making God out to be a liar.
The splendid appearance of being a good fellow cannot hide the
wretch he is. His own conscience agrees with the verdict of God.

> This is the verdict: Light has come into the world, but men loved
> darkness instead of light because their deeds were evil. —John
> 3:19.

Now the other man stands in judgment. He has been arrested in
his mad, evil course, caught red-handed and brought before the
court. The charges are read. He is silent. It is the silence of guilt.
The sentence is passed upon his sins, a judgment as weighty as
God's intense hatred of evil and his intense hatred of God. But
then he sees that God has outwitted his bitter alienation and done
the amazing, undreamed-of thing. The Judge has borne the sen-

tence Himself. In surprise the man exclaims, "He loved me and gave Himself for me!" He believes the gospel, and God gives His verdict: "No charge! In the eyes of this court this man is all that a man should be. The doing and dying of My Son are all counted as his, and for this reason I see him as a whole, holy, healthy man. I therefore declare him righteous."

> To the man who does not work but trusts God who justifies the wicked, his faith is credited as righteousness. — Romans 4:5.

God's verdict is just, and to this the believing sinner's conscience agrees (Hebrews 9:14). Before, his conscience condemned him. He was alienated from himself and filled with self-contempt and self-shame. He had no rest because he could not forgive and accept himself. Nor could he silence his own judgment against himself. But a court higher than his conscience sits and, because of Christ's blood, grants him pardon. "What! Does the Almighty accept me?" he asks in surprise. "Does He see me in the light of the glistening purity of His Son? Yes indeed. I believe it. No more do I stand accused by my conscience. It must bow before the highest court" (1 John 3:19, 20).

Human life and experience are full of instances where a man or woman, boy or girl is profoundly affected by the love and high esteem of another. What of the person who stands in faith before God fully known and fully forgiven? He can see himself in an altogether new light. There is no need for masquerades, masks, the weary round of self-justification. Away with "identity crisis," "self-actualization" and all other attempts to define self-value! God Himself has defined man's value — the value of Christ Himself. The value is not in the believer but in the One to whom he is related. He is liberated.

> Long my imprisoned spirit lay
> Fast bound in sin and nature's night;
> Thine eye diffused a quickening ray;
> I woke, the dungeon flamed with light,
> My chains fell off, my heart was free;
> I rose, went forth, and followed Thee.[3]

The effect of God's justifying verdict is more than a psychological, moral influence. The moment He declares the believing sinner righteous, He treats him as righteous. He sends His Spirit into the believer's heart to witness that he is a son of God (Romans 8:16). He is not only forgiven, but renewed and born again. He can see both the nature and place of the kingly treasure (John 3:3). It is perfect righteousness, total health, abundant life, and it is found in Christ alone.

> And this is the testimony: God has given us eternal life, and this life is in His Son. He who has the Son has life; he who does not have the Son of God does not have life. —1 John 5:11, 12.

---

3. Charles Wesley, "Amazing Love."

8

The Gift of Life

In our pursuit of life we found that:

1. Life is being truly human.

2. Life is being rightly related to God, ourselves, others and the environment.

3. Life is being whole—physically, socially and spiritually. It is total health.

4. Life is total compliance with the whole law of God in our physical, social and spiritual relationships.

At first the law may have seemed easy enough. In fact, learning about eating and sunning ourselves and getting fit was fun. But when we reached right mental attitude and saw what we ought to be and must be to have total health, we were tempted to say, "Let's turn back and settle for something easy like deep breathing or running around the block." But health means wholeness—all or not at all. We had come to the great mountain called Sinai, which was impossible to climb. It was dark as we faced that awful chasm called alienation. There was no way across and we could not turn back.

Then we heard good news. The gospel revealed a Man who was all that we ought to be:

1. He was truly human, the one true specimen of humanity.

2. He was rightly related to God, man, the world and Himself, for He had no conscience of wrong.

3. He was whole — physically, socially and spiritually.

4. His was a life of total compliance with the law of God in all His relationships.

Jesus Christ was life and righteousness and total health. He was all this for us. He was our "ought." In the judgment of God He became what we actually are so that we could stand in the judgment of God as He was — and is. His love made the great exchange, and by faith, given by His grace, we accepted it.

God now sees us and judges us on the basis of what Christ is on our behalf. In this divine judgment or estimation we are:

1. Truly human.

2. Rightly related to God, man and the world.

3. Whole — wholesome, holy, healthy.

4. In harmony with His law — justified.

We have all this by faith. We say *by faith* because perfect health, wholeness, holiness, absolute harmony with God's perfect law, is not in us but in Christ. It is like a fabulous inheritance given to a child. It is not yet his in actual possession, but it will be when he reaches adulthood. Yet it is his even while he waits for it. He can live in the security and the dignity of knowing this. He can even draw upon the inheritance for his present needs. So it is with this life which God has actually given us in Christ. It is reserved for us at God's right hand, and when Christ comes again He will bring it to us (Colossians 3:4). There shall be a great resurrection. This mortal shall put on immortality (1 Corinthians 15:53-55). "We shall be like Him" (1 John 3:2). This will be no phantom existence. Even the environment will be restored, and we will then be in the ideal relationship with God, with the community and with nature itself (Romans 8:18-25; Revelation 21, 22). But faith even now possesses this future because it has been secured by what Christ has already done.

What then constitutes total health? It is salvation of the whole person. It is eternal life — life in its fullness, life without end, life as God meant it to be. It is God's gift. We may have it by faith. To have faith is to have life and righteousness and total health. Paul summarized it all when he said, "He who by faith is righteous shall live" (Romans 1:17, R.S.V.).

So, my friends, we may have eternal life now. It doesn't matter how old we are or how sick we are or how bad we are. It doesn't matter what our past has been. We may have eternal life now — if we believe. "And this is the testimony: God has given us eternal life, and this life is in His Son" (1 John 5:11).

Faith at Work

When we began our pursuit of life, we eagerly heard all the good advice on what to eat, how to exercise and how to have a right mental attitude. And doing these things is beneficial. But all our efforts to secure life proved as useless as climbing a molehill to reach the moon. At the moment of our despair the gospel caught us up, not to the moon, but to the judgment bar of God. There we saw ourselves sitting with Christ, with the free gift of life lavished on miserable, undeserving, alienated sinners. The best things in life are free, and the best of all is the freest of all.

This does not mean we have nothing to do. God made man to be His co-worker. His love is not lavished upon us to make us slothful. It inspires us to know that our work will not be in vain. If God graciously accepts us as being ideal sons, that is what we will strive to be. He sends His Spirit into our hearts and sends us down to earth with work to do. But it is a different kind of work. It is not work on our own account. How can we work for something we already have? If we have been accepted and given life, we don't have to work for it.

The whole world is divided into two classes. The great majority work and strive and toil to be accepted. This burning human passion drives them on. But the road is all uphill. They are anxious, worried, guilty, full of self-doubt. In the end they are either deluded or utterly despondent. They either think they have arrived or they realize they cannot reach their goal. For some the tension becomes so great they break under the strain.

We too are called to work and strive and toil. But we may now do it because we are accepted. We can take up life's burden with a new attitude. This makes the yoke easy and the burden light (Matthew 11:28-30). We are not to work toward acceptance but from acceptance. Because God defines our value, we can run life's race with joy and confidence.

In bringing this good news the Spirit of God gives us a whole new attitude. It is faith. What a person believes at the center of his existence determines his actions, good or bad. Faith, planted in the heart by the gospel, becomes active in love to heal all our relationships (Galatians 5:6).

Believing what God has done for us in Christ, our hearts now begin to give Him His worth. That is to say, we give glory to Him. This means loyalty, submission, reverence and devotion. Worship means giving God His worth rather than going about to establish our own. This is faith working by love. It takes us out of ourselves and into God — to go His way and not our own.

> This is love for God: to obey His commands. And His commands are not burdensome, for everyone born of God has overcome the world. This is the victory that has overcome the world, even our faith. — 1 John 5:3, 4.

The apostle John frequently uses two expressions: keeping God's commandments and loving our brother. They generally mean the same thing. God is so unselfish that He wants our service not for Himself but for our brother. God is gratefully served only by helping our brother.

Without faith it is impossible to really love our brother. The meaning of the word *love* has become so corrupted that its fuss-less, unsentimental, New Testament meaning often escapes us. Good intentions, warm feelings, and sentimental platitudes on nostalgic occasions are only flattering substitutes for the real thing. Although feelings may sometimes accompany it, love which grows out of faith is not a feeling at all. It is a principle of action.

Without faith in our dignity and value with God we will only use our brother to establish our own value. Helping him will be merely a means of proving our own worth. "Saving souls" will be like getting scalps for the Lord. Only the Lord knows how many white headhunters have roamed around Africa. Splendid charity can easily become a splendid idol or status symbol. Faith alone can make the Christian free —free for his brother, free to give and hope for nothing again and to forget himself in the giving.

Faith works in our unconditional acceptance of people, whether they please us or not — whether they follow our ways, belong to our party or are on our side. We cannot love any man unless we love every man without distinction, for love is absolutely impartial.[1] If we think God's acceptance of us is based on something in us, we cannot accept people unconditionally. The moment we define the terms for accepting ourselves, we define the terms for accepting others.

We cannot love others in a godly way unless we love them God's way — unconditionally —just as He loves us. If we do not accept people God's way, how can it be a loving way? For God is love.

We cannot forgive in a godly way until we have accepted God's forgiveness. Realizing that our fellowship with Him is based on continual forgiveness, we can relate to our brother on the basis of forgiveness. This does not mean moral indifference. We may not approve his actions, but his value as a human being is defined by the cross of Christ. Because we ourselves have been freed of a great debt, faith works to make us tolerant and magnanimous. We will not be short on mercy to others if we believe we have been saved by overwhelming mercy.

Faith also works to heal our relationship with the material environment. But some may reason, "If health is God's gift by faith, does complying with the laws of health really matter? Why give up those darling indulgences which injure our bodies? By complying with sensible breathing, drinking, eating, exercising, resting and moderate habits, we may add three or five or ten years to our lives. But by believing the gospel, God will add eternity! What are ten years compared to eternity? Why bother with a single decade?"

What shall we say to this reasoning?

1. Those who are righteous by faith will strive to be righteous in practice. Righteousness embraces all the relationships of human existence. It means fulfilling the obligations of all rela-

---

1. We are not talking about affections.

tionships. Earth and the animals are man's responsibilities. God gave him dominion over the earth to act toward it as God would act toward it, to care for it as God's gift. The Bible says that a just man cares for the life of his beast (Proverbs 12:10). The God who notices the sparrow fall and who clothes the lily with beauty is not indifferent to the way we treat the earth. Nor is He indifferent to the way we treat the body, which is called "the temple of God," "fearfully and wonderfully made" (2 Corinthians 6:16; Psalm 139:14, K.J.V.).

2. Christians are commanded to follow after holiness (Hebrews 12:14). This includes the body (1 Thessalonians 5:23). Holiness is closely related to wholeness. In Old Testament times anything which destroyed the wholeness of human life and tended to death was counted as defilement. Disease is an enemy in God's creation. It is our responsibility to do all in our power to ward it off. The commandment declares, "You shall not kill." This means we should reverence rather than destroy human life. Unfortunately, too many Christians have separated body and soul. The body has often been treated as a sack of dung, and the world has been treated with indifference as if this indifference were a sign of spirituality. This "Grecian" spirituality has led to a world-denying, dehumanizing view of Christian existence. Non-Christians have thus been given a distorted view of the gospel and an unattractive view of God's salvation.

3. The indivisible oneness of the human person means we cannot impair one relationship without impairing all relationships. If we injure our physical health, we diminish our social and spiritual health.

4. The law of life may be summarized, "Love the Lord your God with all your heart, with all your soul, with all your mind and with all your strength" and "your neighbor as yourself" (Mark 12:30, 31). Since we are on this earth to serve God and neighbor to the best of our ability, we sin against both if we neglect our physical habits.

Receiving total health as a free gift will not make compliance with sensible living habits irrelevant or unnecessary. On the contrary, practicing the principles of health will be seen as a privilege and responsibility. The laws of life are God's laws. Gratitude for His gift of life will be manifest by respect for all His laws of life.

The ten laws of life provided good advice. But in the end the good advice will accomplish little without the good news of Jesus Christ. This good news will be of greater benefit than all the good advice. Without the good news we are like the farmer who saw no need to buy a book on good farming. "Look," he reasoned, "what's the use of all that good advice? I'm not farming now half as well as I know how." But the good news will give us willing hands and feet and a ready heart to carry out the good advice.

In this life of faith we are not left to our own resources to fulfill our new resolutions. The Holy Spirit is given to dwell with all God's children. He renews and transforms our hearts so that we want to live as man was meant to live. He gives us strength to move in this new direction. This is a foretaste of the life we have in Christ. In this present life we realize it only in part. But that part is the pledge and guarantee of the whole.

We have seen how faith works in our relationship with God, with others and with the environment. Now, how does faith work in our relation to the self? The answer can be summarized in two words: Forget it! This is life indeed!

9

The Race of Life

Coming to faith did not mean we ended our journey. But it gave us a heart to run and put wings on our feet. Now we are running for a different reason, and the prospects are not uncertain. With Paul we can say, "I do not run like a man running aimlessly" (1 Corinthians 9:26). The writer to the Hebrews exhorts us, "Let us run with perseverance the race marked out for us" (Hebrews 12:1). To those who keep the faith the promise is, "They shall run and not be weary, they shall walk and not faint" (Isaiah 40:31).

It will pay us to spend some time talking about keeping the faith. Faith came to us as we heard the gospel message (Romans 10:17). If we are to keep the faith, we need to keep hearing that same gospel message. This means that we need to regularly read the Bible ourselves, and we need to regularly hear the gospel being proclaimed. Faith does not come to us independently of others, but the message of Christ is mediated to us by other believers. We need to fellowship with those who have come to faith and who regularly gather to hear the gospel preached. A burning ember soon goes out if isolated from the mass of burning embers.

Two dangers confront those who would keep the faith: false expectations and discouragement.

False Expectations

When we reflect on ourselves, we see the self in two ways: as it ought to be and as it actually is. God bridges this gulf by the forgiveness of sins and Christ's righteousness, which are ours by faith. At the same time, God gives us His Spirit for inner renewal and outward reformation. These are evidences that we have come to faith. So with God's help we set out to become what we ought to be. That is the way it should be. If a man doesn't want to become what he ought to be, we fear he does not have the Spirit of God, who always creates a burning desire to be everything we ought to be.

Some, however, are led to entertain false expectations, especially if they have had a glorious awakening to faith. With such a bright new beginning they imagine that all their "enemies" are slain. With God's Spirit, with their own endeavors, or both, they think they can bridge the gulf between what they ought to be and what they are. Of course, they are thankful for God's forgiveness to get them started. But if they avoid self-hypocrisy, they will get a clearer and clearer picture of the length and breadth of the law's requirements and of what God would like them to be. The perception of the "ought" will sharpen. And although growing in faith, the faster they run, the further they will see themselves from the goal. Besides, there are no degrees of righteousness with God. Their righteousness must be entire, wanting nothing, or the gap remains as wide as ever. Apart from the forgiveness of sins there is no difference with God between the best man and the worst man on earth.

As we run the way of faith, let us not entertain the expectation that the tension between the "ought" and reality will lessen because we are improving. This tension becomes greater. The man who has run the furthest and climbed the highest in the way of faith will be most conscious of the distance between what he ought to be and what he is. He will rest more on God's mercy and forgiveness and will smile at the idea that forgiveness is only for beginners.

Nevertheless, it makes a difference whether we run toward high attainments or sit on the road. Keeping the faith is like riding a bicycle. If we don't go on, we fall off. But it is better to lose life itself than to lose the faith. There are unlimited possibilities of self-improvement to the glory of God and the blessing of our fellow men. There is no limit to the usefulness of one who forgets himself and gives himself to be used by the Spirit. This world has been blessed by giants of faith. But ask where they put their faith, and they will point to the blood of Christ. Ask whether they are any nearer what they ought to be, and they will groan or laugh aloud.

Yet for all this, some people continue inventing new techniques whereby they think they can influence an all-powerful God to put an end to the human abyss. They want to show by their rounded personalities or their charismatic blessings what God can do for the rest of mankind. Then when they find that God does not cooperate with their excessive zeal, they often fall into discouragement or desperation.

It is sufficient to live by the remedy we found at the first. It will surely be sufficient till the last. And if there be any difference, it is this: We will feel our need of mercy at the end more than we did at the beginning. The wholeness of life teaches us that we cannot be fully restored in any dimension of life until we are restored in every dimension. Since we are part of the community of faith, a community likened to a body (1 Corinthians 12:12,13), we cannot run ahead and become perfect until the whole body of believers becomes perfect together (Hebrews 11:39, 40).

In the final analysis the decisive thing will not be how far we have run or how high we have climbed, but only, have we kept the faith?

If it were good for us and for God's glory, He could turn us into saints as pure and glistening as the angels in the twinkling of an eye. Why doesn't He use His power to make us, at least in soul — character, mind — all that we ought to be?[1]

1. It is an exhibition of His wisdom. It is good for our faith. It keeps us running after His mercy, gives us more sympathy with fellow sinners and makes us long for our Lord's return.

2. It is an exhibition of His power. He keeps us righteous in His

---

1. Why not include the whole man? How we unconsciously make the unholy (unhealthy, unwhole, unwholesome) proposition of separating body from soul!

sight while we are still sinners in ourselves.

3. It is an exhibition of His mercy. If God made us perfect and left us in this fallen world, we would suffer hell. Christ's suffering in this fallen world was beyond imagination. God would spare us from that.

4. We will add what the Bible teaches: In this life we can be righteous before God only by faith (Romans 1:17; 3:20; Psalm 143:2; Galatians 5:5).

Some, seeing they cannot resolve the tension between what they ought to be and what they actually are, try to solve the problem by getting rid of the law. "You don't need the law if you have faith!" they cry. They may even sing the good old song, "Free from the law, O happy condition." But what do they mean by "free from the law"? If they mean free from its penalty or from trying to get life by keeping it, they are right. But if they mean that faith frees us from the law as a rule of duty, they are wrong. The law is the "ought." It is the will of God. It is all that we should do. There is law in the New Testament as well as in the Old. "Be forgiving!" "Love your enemies!" "Carry one another's burdens!" "Be humble like Jesus Christ!" "Speak evil of no one!" are some of the many "oughts" in Paul's letters. The man who says, "I live by no law," has made an impossible law — to live by no law. If he obeyed this law, his life would be an unplanned, disorganized blot without order or meaning. Life is like a poem to be composed or a canvas to be painted. There must be form. While love is the principle of all obedience to God, law gives love its form. Unless the law of Christian duty is kept before us, we will take forgiveness for granted and will feel that we scarcely need it at all. The life of faith does not presume on God's mercy. Faith cannot exist with an evil intention to ignore the will of God.

The path of faith is straight. But on either side is a deep ditch for those who lose the faith. On one side is the error of thinking we can be saved by splendid attainments. On the other side is the error of believing we can be saved while disobeying the express will of God.

This means that those who run the way of faith have two distinguishing attitudes. Because God honored His law at Calvary, they too respect the laws of life. But also because of Calvary, they believe their righteousness with God is by faith alone.

Discouragement

When we fall let us remember that we are still in God's favor if we are still in the faith. Let us get up and go on because God is for us and His Spirit is with us. His promise is sure: "Never will I leave you; never will I forsake you" (Hebrews 13:5). God never runs out of mercy, so let us keep the faith. We may be down, but we are never out if only we keep the faith. In the final analysis the decisive thing will not be how often we slipped or fell, but did we keep the faith? For faith, faith alone, is our righteousness (Romans 4:5) because it lays hold of Christ, who is pleasing to God. This is life — to live by faith.

We should not make our experience the center of our attention. While honesty and some self-examination are in order, we must not dwell on our failures and shortcomings. It is a law of the mind that whatever gets our attention gets us. We should not even dwell on our good experiences and make them the center of our concern or Christian witness. We must not dwell on God's gifts so much that we forget the Giver. Dwelling on one's spiritual experience is a cause of much discouragement.

Do you remember ever trying to balance a broom on your finger? When you kept your eyes on the top of the broom, all would go well. But the moment you started watching your finger, the broom would fall over.

In the same way, we must keep our eyes on what Christ has done for us and what He is to us at God's right hand. When we believe this with all our hearts, His Spirit works in us — unconsciously. Someone once put it this way: "I looked at Christ and the Dove of peace flew into my heart. I looked at the Dove and it flew away."

Let us remember that the decisive thing is not how thrilling or how mundane or even how baffling our experience in running this race has been. It is only this one question that matters: Have we kept the faith?

10

The Celebration of Life

At the beginning of our journey we set out in pursuit of life. We resolved to take it by storm. That is the parable of human nature itself. Everyone is in search of life. Hopefully, our journey made us realize that we could not find life. It lay beyond, above us like a dark mystery. Between it and us was a frightful abyss we could not cross. The truth then came to us—we did not come to it. Life had really come in pursuit of us and used our foolish dreams to draw us to Itself. For Life is Christ, and Christ is our Life (Philippians 1:21; Colossians 3:4). Life found us and, because Life is love, gave Itself to us until It had nothing more to give. "Son," Life said, "take Me and live." Life came to us not by our own noble exploits nor by our irreverently snatching It. It came as a Gift to be taken freely or not at all. And because It is a Gift, It calls us to the spirit of grateful celebration.

To the men who wrote the Old Testament, life was not something to be endured but to be celebrated. Life was a great boon. To live was to live in praise and celebration of what God had done (Isaiah 38:18,19). Those who did not participate in this celebration could be counted as dead even while they lived. But this Old Testament celebration was not the celebration of religious mystics who think worship means to be lifted out of the body and the evil, smelly world to become pure spirit, a vapor which vanishes

into nothingness. No! No! The men of the Old Testament may
have had their faith in heaven, but they had their feet on earth.
Their celebration was celebration in and with the community.
They knew that no man could be whole while alone. They did not
look upon this earth as "worldly" as many religious people do
today. Life was to be celebrated with eating, drinking, marrying
(Proverbs 5:18; Song of Solomon), rearing children, planting
vineyards and eating their fruit, with toiling and rejoicing to see
the light of the sun. They could see that the whole order had been
disrupted by this foreign thing called sin. They knew that the
earth sometimes bleeds in pain. But they had a faith founded on
the conviction that God had acted, God was acting, and God would
act in the fullness of time to make all things new (Isaiah 65:17;
66:22).

God did not disappoint their faith. "When the time had fully
come" (Galatians 4:4), God acted in Christ to reconcile the world
to Himself (Romans 5:10), to remove every barrier that would
prevent Him from pouring His love upon the world so that men
might have life and have it to the full (John 10:10). Christ has
become the watershed of history. Every time men write the date
they unconsciously acknowledge that time is measured in reference to Him. History is now *His story,* a story which judges every
man. What God has done in giving us His Son is so great that the
old songs of celebration will never do. "And they sang a new song."
"Let us rejoice and be glad" (Revelation 5:9; 19:7). God's secret is
out. The tomb is empty. Christ is risen from the dead, having
taken away the sting of death. Victory has already taken place.
The future is a foregone conclusion.

The gospel is an invitation to a great party. There is no other
like this, for God has prepared it Himself. The pleasure is His. The
surprise is ours. This party is not a dinner where only the great
and the beautiful gather while the rest watch in envy. Having
lavished His table with the accumulated love of eternity, He
Himself, in His gospel, appeals for men to come. He delights in
calling those who are least deserving, those who know they can
never repay what He has done. The Almighty Creator wants to
celebrate with poor, lost men and women, those who realize they
are undeserving. If some are too proud to eat with "tax collectors
and sinners" (Matthew 9:11), God is not too proud — or too holy.
God is no snob. While many "good" people think that being good

leads to fellowship with God, He turns them upside down by showing that fellowship leads to goodness. He meets sinners where they are. The All-Holy comes to fellowship with the unholy. Divine love always breaks through our petty notions of what God ought to do. He will not be the God of the status quo. He insists on doing the surprising, undreamed-of thing. Divine love offers acceptance to men just as they are. But if they accept it they cannot remain just as they are. Overwhelmed by divine love, they will be reconciled to the life God has planned for them.

As we remember what God has done and what has been given us, life becomes a celebration. Living by faith is not preoccupation with ourselves or exploring our psyche. It is forgetting ourselves and celebrating.

Faith is the attitude of celebration. It is not dreaming that the world is all lovely. It isn't. Rather, it is to live in the conviction that this universe will ultimately prove both just and friendly. Of course, we now see the cruel inequities and injustices of life. Cheats often prosper and crooked men reach the top. Truth is forever on the scaffold and error ever on the throne. Yet we know with the poet that that "scaffold sways the future." Justice will be done. Faith sees that the universe is also friendly. It is for us because "God is for us" (Romans 8:31). This is not to deny that the universe can present a savage face. Volcanoes bury a village, and terrorism and torture reveal man's inhumanity to man. But faith looks beyond and says, "Since God is there, the universe will prove friendly in the end."

This faith shares in the faith of Him who came to this earth and was met by failure at every turn. There was no room for Him in the inn, no room for Him in His own country though only a babe, no room for Him in the hearts of His own people. The Lord of glory was He, but He trod this world unrecognized, unhonored, with nowhere to lay His head. "He came to that which was His own, but His own did not receive Him." "He was despised and rejected by men" (John 1:11; Isaiah 53:3). But He would not fail nor be discouraged. He put His faith in God and pressed on alone. The storm grew black around Him. Men returned Him evil for good. His friends forsook Him. One betrayed Him. Another denied Him. He was spat on, mocked and derided. Even God seemed to forsake Him. His death appeared the greatest failure and disaster any man had ever faced — until God showed His side of the story.

Faith, therefore, is only possible because it is sustained by His. If we keep the faith, our lives will also be a glorious triumph, not seen to be such here, but seen to be such when God lets us see His side of the story.

The cross stands as the immovable landmark of all history, inspiring us to believe that the universe is both just and friendly. If it were only just, it would destroy us. For we deserve death. If it were only friendly and indifferent to good and bad, it would be a monstrous place to live. But Calvary declares that God will see justice done. The rule of His law shall prevail. And Calvary also declares that the Sovereign of the universe is friendly. He is even friendly enough to sorrowfully let a man have his own way when he says, "No thank you, I don't want your Christ."

With faith in such a universe we can be optimistic. The world is disintegrating. Men are losing all hope in the future. Like Louis XV, statesmen are saying, "After me the deluge." Men are losing faith in each other. It is starkly evident that without faith among men the social order disintegrates. But faith in Christ enables us to believe in our fellow men and relate to them in optimism and hope. Faith is not embittered when the giving of ourselves seems to be spurned. Christ says, "Whatever you did, . . . you did for Me" (Matthew 25:40).

Faith that the universe is not ultimately hostile makes us friends of the earth, not looking on soil and tree and animal as things to exploit, but to nurture. Faith reconciles us to our inseparable identity with the earth and all creatures great and small. It inspires us to regard the earth as something to be cared for and enjoyed. Like ourselves it is not yet what it ought to be. But with us it hastens to meet our common destiny when God at last says, "Behold, I make all things new."

Appendix

Section One

Healthful Habits

Many think health is the result of chance or accident. But a number of studies have shown that health risks are related to personal health habits.

A nine-year study of 7,000 adult residents of Alameda County, California, was begun in 1965.[1] It showed that seven health practices were closely related to both death rate and health status.[2] Forty-five-year-old men observing six or seven of these health practices could expect to live 11 years longer than men the same age with fewer than four health practices. Forty-five-year-old women with six or seven health practices could expect to live seven years longer than women the same age with fewer than four health practices.[3] Even more astounding, 45-year-old men or women with all seven health habits could expect the health status —general health and feeling of well-being—of teenagers practicing only two habits or less.[4]

How do you measure up? On the following health habit checklist, give yourself one point for each health habit you practice. Use the overweight table on page 108 to determine if you are less than 20% overweight.

---

1. "Health and Ways of Living Study" (Berkeley: Human Population Laboratory, California State Department of Public Health, 1976).

2. Belloc and Breslow, "Health Status and Health Practices," pp. 409-21; Belloc, "Health Practices and Mortality," pp. 67-81; idem, *Health Practices and Mortality — Nine-Year Follow-up: Paper Comparing the Results of the 5½-Year Follow-up of Respondents in the Health and Ways of Living Study in 1965 with the Results of the 9-Year Follow-up Completed in 1974* (Berkeley: Human Population Laboratory, California State Department of Public Health, 1976).

3. Belloc, "Health Practices and Mortality," pp. 67-81.

4. Computed on nine-year follow-up data from the Health and Ways of Living Study, kindly provided in personal communication by Dr. James Wylie, Human Population Laboratory, California State Department of Public Health, Berkeley, California, 1976.

Health Habit Checklist

1. Air	☐ I do not smoke.
2. Water	☐ I seldom or never have more than four alcoholic drinks per sitting.
3. Food	☐ I eat a substantial breakfast every day or almost every day.
4. Exercise	☐ I take long walks or engage in sports, swimming, gardening or other physical activity at least three times a week.
5. Rest	☐ I regularly have seven or eight hours of sleep.
6. Regularity	☐ I seldom or never eat between meals.
7. Moderation	☐ I weigh less than 20% above my desired weight. (See overweight table.)
Total Number of Health Habits I Practice	☐ (Number of *true* statements)

Overweight Table

Height (Inches)	Overweight Limit (Pounds)	
	Men	Women
60		130
61		133
62		136
63		139
64	156	144
65	160	149
66	164	155
67	169	160
68	174	165
69	180	169
70	185	174
71	190	
72	195	
73	200	
74	205	
75	212	

Health Status Age

Good health status is a feeling of well-being and freedom from illness and disability. Your health age is the age of the average person with your health status. You can find your health status age by using the chart on page 110. Here is how:

1. At the top, circle the number of health habits you found that you practice.

2. At the left-hand side, circle your age group.

3. Draw a horizontal line from your age group to the column below the number of health habits you circled.

4. Note the number at the intersection.

5. If it has a plus (+) sign before it, add this number to your actual age to find your health age.

6. If it has a minus (−) sign before it, subtract this number from your actual age to find your health age.

Health Status Ages for Men and Women

Age	0-2 Habits	3 Habits	4 Habits	5 Habits	6 Habits	7 Habits
20-24	+14.3	+ 7.4	+ 0.5	−1.1	−4.2	− 9.4
25-29	+15.6	+ 8.3	+ 1.8	−0.9	−4.5	−10.2
30-34	+16.9	+ 9.1	+ 3.0	−0.6	−4.7	−11.1
35-39	+18.2	+ 9.9	+ 4.2	−0.4	−5.0	−12.0
40-44	+19.4	+10.7	+ 5.4	−0.1	−5.2	−12.9
45-49	+20.7	+11.6	+ 6.7	+0.1	−5.5	−13.8
50-54	+22.0	+12.4	+ 7.9	+0.3	−5.7	−14.7
55-59	+23.3	+13.2	+ 9.1	+0.6	−6.0	−15.5
60-64	+24.5	+14.0	+10.4	+0.8	−6.2	−16.4
65-69	+25.8	+14.8	+11.6	+1.1	−6.5	−17.3
70-74	+27.1	+15.7	+12.8	+1.3	−6.8	−18.2

This exercise teaches us something important about a true philosophy of life. Compliance with the laws of life promotes both quality and length of life. Noncompliance invites disease and hastens death.

Section Two

Healthful Deep Breathing

Upper Lungs   Lower Lungs

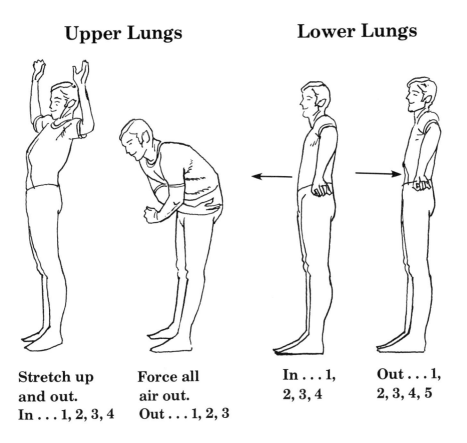

Stretch up   Force all   In . . . 1,   Out . . . 1,
and out.   air out.   2, 3, 4   2, 3, 4, 5
In . . . 1, 2, 3, 4   Out . . . 1, 2, 3

Practice this for three minutes morning and evening. Develop the habit of regular deep breathing. Good breathing habits require good posture.

Section Three

Healthful Weight

The following tables assume height and weight taken with shoes and indoor clothing. A small frame means thin chest, narrow shoulders and narrow pelvis. A large frame means thick chest, broad shoulders and broad pelvis.

Desirable Weights for Men and Women Aged 25 and Over[5]
(in pounds according to height and frame)

Men (with 1-inch heels)

Height		Small Frame	Medium Frame	Large Frame
Feet	Inches			
5	2	112-120	118-129	126-141
5	3	115-123	121-133	129-144
5	4	118-126	124-136	132-148
5	5	121-129	127-139	135-152
5	6	124-133	130-143	138-156
5	7	128-137	134-147	142-161
5	8	132-141	138-152	147-166
5	9	136-145	142-156	151-170
5	10	140-150	146-160	155-174
5	11	144-154	150-165	159-179
6	0	148-158	154-170	164-184
6	1	152-162	158-175	168-189
6	2	156-167	162-180	173-194
6	3	160-171	167-185	178-199
6	4	164-175	172-190	182-204

5. Adapted from Metropolitan Life Insurance Co., *Statistical Bulletin* 40 (Nov.-Dec. 1959): 3.

Women (with 2-inch heels)

Height		Small Frame	Medium Frame	Large Frame
Feet	Inches			
4	10	92- 98	96-107	104-119
4	11	94-101	98-110	106-122
5	0	96-104	101-113	109-125
5	1	99-107	104-116	112-128
5	2	102-110	107-119	115-131
5	3	105-113	110-122	118-134
5	4	108-116	113-126	121-138
5	5	111-119	116-130	125-142
5	6	114-123	120-135	129-146
5	7	118-127	124-139	133-150
5	8	122-131	128-143	137-154
5	9	126-135	132-147	141-158
5	10	130-140	136-151	145-163
5	11	134-144	140-155	149-168
6	0	138-148	144-159	153-173

Section Four

Healthful Diet

The following table shows important changes which need to be made in the typical Western diet to make it more healthful. For example, most people should nearly double their intake of vegetables and should eat much less salt and salty foods.[6]

---

6. C.F. Church and H.N. Church, *Food Values of Portions Commonly Used,* 12th ed. (Philadelphia: J.B. Lippincott Co., 1975), p. 186; "A National Nutrition Policy: Current and Emerging Issues," *Dairy Council Digest* 48 (Nov.-Dec. 1977): 31-6; Select Committee on Nutrition and Human Needs, U.S. Senate, *Dietary Goals for the United States* (Washington, D.C.: U.S. Government Printing Office, 1977).

Double — **Fresh Vegetables**
(green leafy vegetables, potatoes and other root vegetables; peas, beans and other legumes)
For flavoring, preferably use vegetable oils and cream sparingly rather than butter, lard or suet.

**Eat
More**

**Fresh Fruit
Whole Grains**
(bread, cereals, macaroni)

Skim or nonfat milk, buttermilk and cottage cheese

**Average
Diet**

Whole milk, cream, butter, cheese and eggs

Red meats
(beef, mutton, etc.)
Further reduce total fat by avoiding such animal fats as lard, drippings and fatty cuts of meat. Partly replace these foods with nuts and vegetable oils containing more polyunsaturated fats.

**Eat
Less**

Refined and processed sugars

Salt, salty foods and spices

Coffee, tea, cola drinks and alcoholic beverages

None

Section Five

Healthful Posture

Standing

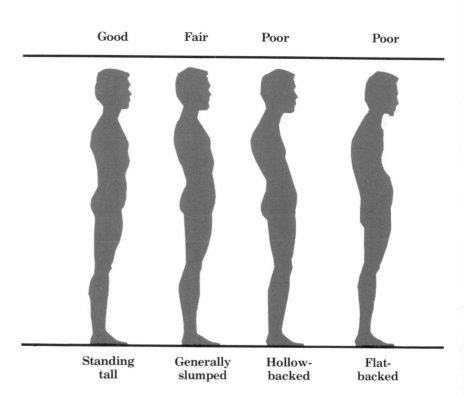

Good	Fair	Poor	Poor
Standing tall	Generally slumped	Hollow-backed	Flat-backed

Lifting and Carrying

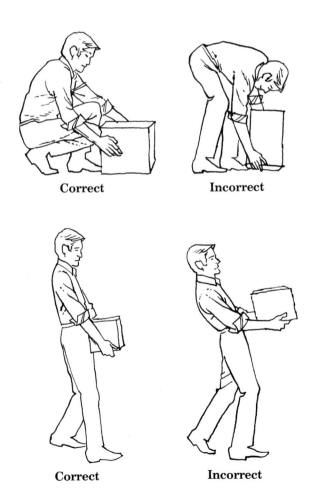

Correct   Incorrect

Correct   Incorrect

Section Six

Healthful Exercise

Exercise is essential to give strength and endurance to both the heart and the muscles of the skeleton. Someone has said that your heart is only as strong as the calves of your legs.

Many popular books give detailed instructions on how to achieve and maintain physical fitness with various kinds of exercise. But a brisk three-mile walk in 36-44 minutes, taken five times a week, will keep most people physically fit.[7]

Before beginning an exercise program, you should consult a physician, particularly if you are over 30 or have a medical problem such as heart trouble, diabetes, high blood pressure, high blood cholesterol, overweight, asthma, emphysema, arthritis, rheumatism, gout, leg cramps, shortness of breath, stiff muscles or joints, or a heavy tobacco-smoking habit.

If you are over 35 and have not been exercising, you should begin with a 15-minute one-mile walk five times a week. Gradually extend the distance and increase your speed until you reach a pace of three miles in 36-44 minutes in 16 weeks.[8] If you are under 35 or have already been exercising regularly, you can reach your intended pace more quickly.[9]

Observe the following precautions throughout your exercise program:

---

7. Kenneth H. Cooper, *Aerobics* (New York: Bantam Books, 1968); idem, *The New Aerobics* (New York: Bantam Books, 1970).

8. Ibid.

9. Ibid.

1. Do not exercise vigorously right after a meal.

2. Preferably, exercise in the open air at a moderate environmental temperature and humidity.

3. Do not overexercise when feeling ill. Return to a lower level of effort following illness.

4. Aching joints and muscles indicate too fast a pace too soon. These pains commonly occur in the first two weeks but normally disappear shortly thereafter.

5. Discontinue exercise and check with a physician if you have any of the following problems during or following exercise:

   a. Chest, tooth, jaw, neck or arm pain.

   b. Difficulty in breathing.

   c. Light-headedness or fainting.

   d. Irregular heart rate.

   e. Severe muscle and joint pain.

   f. Excessive fatigue.

   g. Unexplained weight loss.

   h. Persistent nausea or vomiting.